Personalities and Problems
Interpretive Essays in World Civilizations
Volume One

Personalities and Problems

Interpretive Essays in World Civilizations

Third Edition

VOLUME ONE

Ken Wolf
Murray State University

Boston   Burr Ridge, IL   Dubuque, IA   Madison, WI   New York
San Francisco   St. Louis   Bangkok   Bogotá   Caracas   Kuala Lumpur
Lisbon   London   Madrid   Mexico City   Milan   Montreal   New Delhi
Santiago   Seoul   Singapore   Sydney   Taipei   Toronto

Higher Education

PERSONALITIES AND PROBLEMS: INTERPRETIVE ESSAYS IN WORLD
CIVILIZATIONS, VOLUME I

Published by McGraw-Hill, a business unit of The McGraw-Hill Companies, Inc.,
1221 Avenue of the Americas, New York, NY, 10020. Copyright © 2005, 1999,
1994, by The McGraw-Hill Companies, Inc. All rights reserved. No part of this
publication may be reproduced or distributed in any form or by any means, or
stored in a database or retrieval system, without the prior written consent of The
McGraw-Hill Companies, Inc., including, but not limited to, in any network or
other electronic storage or transmission, or broadcast for distance learning.

Some ancillaries, including electronic and print components, may not be
available to customers outside the United States.

This book is printed on acid-free paper.

1 2 3 4 5 6 7 8 9 0 DOC/DOC 0 9 8 7 6 5 4

ISBN 0–07–256564–0

Publisher: *Lyn Uhl*
Editorial assistant: *Sean Connelly*
Senior marketing manager: *Katherine Bates*
Project manager: *Destiny Rynne Hadley*
Production supervisor: *Janean A. Utley*
Designer: *Cassandra J. Chu*
Associate supplement producder: *Meghan Durko*
Manager, Photo research: *Brian J. Pecko*
Art manager: *Robin K. Mouat*
Art director: *Jeanne M. Schreiber*
Cover design: *Cassandra Chu*
Interior design: *Michael Remener*
Typeface: *10/12 Palatino*
Compositor: *Shepherd-Imagineering Media Services Inc.*
Printer: *R. R. Donnelley and Sons Inc.*

Library of Congress Cataloging-in-Publication Data

Wolf, Ken, 1943–
    Personalities and problems : interpretive essays in world civilizations /
Ken Wolf; illustrations by John Stephen Hatton.—3rd ed.
        p. cm.
    Includes bibliographical references.
    ISBN 0-07-256564-0 (v. 1 : softcover : alk. paper) — ISBN 0-07-256566-7 (v. 2 :
softcover : alk. paper)
    1. Civilization—History. 2. Biography. I. Title.
CB69.W63 2005
909—dc22   2004040189

www.mhhe.com

About the Author

KEN WOLF is Professor of History at Murray State University in Murray, KY, where he has taught since 1969. He was born in Davenport, Iowa, and received his B.A. from St. Ambrose College (1965) and his M.A. and Ph.D. in history from the University of Notre Dame (1966, 1972). Professor Wolf helped design Murray State's required World Civilizations course and has taught it since its inception. He also teaches The Development of Historical Thinking on a regular basis. Professor Wolf has published articles on European nationalism, historiography, intellectual history, and the teaching of history in *The Journal of the History of Ideas, The International Encyclopedia of Social Sciences—Biographical Supplement, Teaching History,* the *Illinois Quarterly, The Journal of Kentucky Studies,* and the *AHA Perspectives.* For five years (1987–1991), Wolf served as one of two deans of the Kentucky Governor's Scholars Program, a state-sponsored summer enrichment program for 700 high-achieving, rising high school seniors and recently helped begin a similar program, known as the Commonwealth Honors Academy, at Murray State. He was selected as a Pew Faculty Fellow in International Affairs for 1993–1994. He and his wife, Deanna, have three children and four grandchildren.

*To my family, my colleagues at Murray State
and
the students, faculty, and staff of the
Commonwealth Honors Academy,
2001–2004*

and to my grandchildren

*for helping me give meaning to the phrase
"life-long learning."*

Contents

Preface   xiii

1. Hammurabi and Moses:
   Law as a Mirror of Civilization   3

   *What do the laws of a society tell us about the lives and beliefs of the
   people who write, enforce, and obey those laws? What was the chief
   difference between the law codes of these two leaders, and what
   caused this?*

2. Zoroaster and Buddha: Explaining Suffering   15

   *Why does evil exist in the world? The "Western" Zoroaster and the
   "Eastern" Buddha answer this question quite differently. What are
   some implications of their answers for our understanding of world
   history?*

3. Confucius and Plato:
   A Few Really Good People   27

   *What is the best way to create a strong society? Can people be led by
   moral example because they are basically good—or do they need a
   philosopher-king to help them control the evil within themselves?*

4. Mahavira and Diogenes: Unconventional Men   39

Can a man challenge the behavior and values of the people in his society and still remain a part of that society? (Or when is a misfit not really a misfit?) Why did self-reliance and individualism take different forms in these Eastern and Western societies? What characteristics did these men share?

5. Thucydides and Sima Qian: Learning from the Past   51

Why do we keep records of the past? How do historical works reflect the values of writers and of their cultures? Is one kind of history better than another?

6. Asoka and Shi Huangdi: Honey and Vinegar   65

Is it more effective to govern people by moral persuasion or by coercion? Can the carrot be effective without the stick?

7. Boudica and Zenobia: Challenging the Romans   77

Why were Roman armies difficult to defeat? What makes female warriors attractive to historians?

8. Irene and Wu Zhao: Two Iconoclasts   91

What qualities do women rulers need to succeed in a society dominated by men? What criteria should be used by historians to evaluate their careers?

9. Al-Ghazali and Aquinas: Faith and Reason   103

What is the proper balance between faith and reason in seeking to understand the Divine? How do two important Christian and Muslim thinkers differ on this question?

10 Marco Polo and Ibn Battuta:
The Merchant and the Pilgrim 115

*How did the predispositions of two famous medieval travelers color
what they reported—and how they reported it? What was the most
important similarity in the stories of these two travelers?*

11. Mansa Musa and Louis IX:
Pilgrims and State-Builders 129

*How did the institution of monarchy differ in Europe and West
Africa in the thirteenth and fourteenth centuries? In a religious age,
does a king show he is powerful by being pious or does his piety help
him become powerful?*

12. Prince Henry and Zheng He: Sailing South 139

*How do the structures and values of a society affect the way
people view contact with other cultures? Why did Europeans
benefit more from the voyages of Prince Henry than the Chinese
did from those of Zheng He?*

13. Erasmus and Luther: The Reformer's Dilemma 149

*To what extent is it possible to reform an institution from within?
What intellectual and personal qualities led Luther to be more
radical than Erasmus? Is is better to promote greater change for
fewer people or less change for more people?*

14. Elizabeth and Akbar: The Religion of the Ruler? 161

*Can a ruler use religious conflict to strengthen his or her own rule?
Can a ruler's religous preference be the basis of unity in a
religiously divided state?*

15. Kangxi and Louis XIV:
Dynastic Rulers, East and West   179

To what extent can dynastic rulers control their own fate? What is the key to successful "absolutism"?

Preface

Dear Reader:

The people you meet in these pages illustrate the richness and variety of human history from the earliest civilizations to the seventeenth century C.E. The personalities range from a key figure in the creation of what we call the Judeo-Christian tradition, Moses, to one of the strongest rulers of modern China, Kangxi. If history is the study of human beings who make it, *Personalities and Problems* is an introduction to world civilizations that focuses upon some of the most interesting men and women which the written records of these civilizations allow us to meet. This book assumes no previous knowledge of history; it does assume that the lives of exciting people have a certain magic that captures our attention across the boundaries of space and time.

But most of you know that history is more (sometimes less) than the study of interesting people. If all the interesting historical figures were included in our history texts, the books would be too large to carry, much less read. The people we choose to include in our histories must also be considered interesting or important—by someone. Whether great in the traditional textbook sense of the term or not, these personalities were included in this work because I found them interesting and thought their lives could help you better understand some of the issues that historians and other scholars have struggled with in their teaching, research, and writing. Before you can assess their importance for yourselves, it will be helpful for you to begin to classify or organize them.

Eight of the people you will meet in these pages were primarily political leaders—people such as Hammurabi, Asoka, and Irene. Another nine were primarily thinkers and/or religious leaders; this list includes Moses, Zoroaster, Buddha, Confucius, Plato, Mahavira, Diogenes, Desiderius Erasmus, and Martin Luther. You will also meet four men best described as explorers: Marco Polo, Ibn Battuta, Prince Henry, and Zheng He. Putting people in such broad categories is, of course, only one way to describe them—and not necessarily the best way. For one thing, in history as in life, people have a way of breaking through our neat categories. Moses, for example, was both a religious leader and a ruler of his people. People such as Asoka, Elizabeth, and Akbar were also rulers who tried to influence the religious lives of their people. In the period before 1500 C.E., in particular, it is very difficult to separate religion and politics. In a larger sense, this book is interdisciplinary; its author is committed to the idea that whatever lines we might draw between subjects in schools, we cannot understand human beings adequately if we separate their political behavior from their religious beliefs, their social position, or their economic concerns.

A second way to classify people is to ask about the impact they made on their society. Some, such as Hammurabi and Mahavira, were important because their actions reflected the dominant values of their society. Others, such as Martin Luther, were significant because they challenged those values. Occasionally, we find people who both reflected the beliefs of their time and place and tried to change the way people thought about the world. Chinese mariner Zheng He did not change the direction of Chinese history in the fifteenth century, but his voyages of exploration offer a fascinating look at what might have been. His counterpart, Prince Henry of Portugal, reflected European attitudes toward overseas exploration and, by his work, helped Europeans become even more outward-looking. Greek Cynic Diogenes and his Indian counterpart, religious reformer Mahavira, challenged people in their respective societies to live up to the standards they professed.

These are only two ways of classifying the personalities in world history. As you read these essays, I invite you to devise some of your own. Your determination of what makes an individual a success or a failure, admirable or deplorable, will necessarily be influenced by your personal values, and those prominent today. I ask, however, that you also consider the times in which these individuals lived, as well as the problems they faced, when judging them. If you consider both their problems and the values they brought to bear in trying to solve them, you will begin the process of thinking historically. You will become historically minded.

To help you with this task, all of these personalities are presented to you in relation to a particular issue or issues that they had to face or that their careers raise for us—as thoughtful citizens of an increasingly interdependent world. These issues—noted by the questions that begin each essay—include such things as the role of religion as a social force, the problems faced by female leaders in male-dominated societies, and the way the structures and values of a society affect the way people feel about contact with other cultures. Also, each personality is paired with a contemporary or near-contemporary who faces a similar problem or issue, either in the same civilization or country or in another one. These pairings are often cross-cultural and should help you understand that human problems really do transcend the boundaries of race, creed, or nation. When we begin to see that individuals as different as Kangxi and Louis XIV had to face similar problems in creating a strong dynastic state, we can appreciate the fact that our history is world history and not only a history of individual nations or even civilizations.

Historical greatness, then, is not just a matter of how talented we are (or how lucky) but also a matter of when and where we live. History helps make us as surely as we help make history, as the careers of the two ancient historians, Thucydides and Sima Qian, illustrate. If this book challenges you to think about just how and why this happens, it will have served its purpose.

Because this book assumes no prior knowledge of history, or even prior college-level work, I use brackets [ ] to define terms which might be unfamiliar to a beginning student. You also should know that each chapter is designed to stand independently; chapters need not be read in order. You can start at any point and read in either direction, after checking with your teacher, of course!

This third edition of *Personalities and Problems* has been modified in direct response to teachers who used earlier editions and requested changes. Chapters removed from this edition to allow space for new ones may be downloaded from the McGraw-Hill World History Website at [www.mhhe.com]. All the remaining chapters have been corrected and new information added where possible. New chapters in this edition respond to readers' requests for more on Rome and a growing student interest in religion. As in the Preface to the first edition, I repeat my invitation to readers to suggest who ought to be included or omitted in any future edition. Your comments have been taken seriously, and will be again, should this work appear in future editions.

In addition to all those hard-working colleagues, Murray State staff, and students whom I thanked in the first and second editions of *Personalities and Problems,* I would like to again thank the teachers in the Department of History, especially Bill Schell and Charlotte Beahan, who remain willing to read and critique my work and whose comments always improve it; and Melinda Grimsley-Smith, whose work as my graduate assistant made the job of revision much easier. I would also like to thank the reviewers of the second edition whose comments helped shape this third edition: Robert Blackey, California State University, San Bernardino; Myles L. Clowers, San Diego City College; Nancy Erickson, Erskine College; Norman O. Forness, Gettysburg College; Paul E. Gill, Shippensburg University; David Grier, Erskine College; Dane Kennedy, University of Nebraska, Lincoln; Fred Nielsen, University of Nebraska, Omaha; Melvin E. Page, East Tennessee University; Jon Stauff, Saint Ambrose University; and Steven F. White, Mount Saint Mary's College. My thanks as well to the fine librarians at Murray State and at the Hesburgh Library in the University of Notre Dame, where I have been privileged to work several summers. Lyn Uhl and her wonderful staff at McGraw-Hill have been very supportive and helpful in suggesting revisions and in surveying users of the first edition. Any errors which remain after all this help can only be due to my own carelessness or stubbornness—and all those mentioned above should be absolved of any errors and credited with trying to save me from myself. We all join, however, in hoping that this work offers you pleasant reading, new insights into the past, and intellectual excitement.

Sincerely,

Ken Wolf

Department of History
Murray State University
Murray, KY 42071

CHAPTER 1

Hammurabi and Moses: Law as a Mirror of Civilization

What do the laws of a society tell us about the lives and beliefs of the people who write, enforce, and obey those laws? What was the chief difference between the law codes of these two leaders, and what caused this?

Early civilizations were both fragile and gradual. We often make lists of their qualities as if they were chemical compounds or recipes: take several Neolithic farming villages and a river valley; add a group of nomadic herdsmen; stir briskly with bronze weapons. Blend in language, writing, a system of class differentiation with warriors and priests at the head of the list, and simmer until cities and civilization emerge. Garnish with trade and conquest before serving.

Of course, it did not happen that way. The ideas, customs, and material things that constituted early civilizations came together slowly over centuries. Only after the fact, when the cities with their kings, priests, beliefs, shops, and soldiers were all in place, do we speak of a particular civilization. And this complex social, political, and economic creation was both strong and weak, strong enough to engage in wars of conquest, weak enough to be destroyed by the death of a powerful leader, or by a famine caused by a drop of two degrees in the average annual mean temperature.

While it lasted, each great early civilization was held together by power and traditions: the power of political and social elites and the traditions which are embodied in the great religious and philosophical value systems that mark all major civilizations.

These traditions that gave meaning to political and social institutions—to family life, education, government, and the marketplace—are reflected in a civilization's laws.

3

We see such reflections in two early, but very different, civilizations in the ancient near east: the Babylonian and the Hebrew. The first developed in the early part of the second millennium B.C.E. in the Tigris and Euphrates valley, while the second came together around the thirteenth century B.C.E. when Moses led the Hebrew people out of Egypt east into the Sinai Desert. The most famous ruler of the Babylonians was Hammurabi, who ruled from 1792–1750 B.C.E. After long wars in which he conquered the older Sumerian cities such as Larsa, Erech, and Ur in the southern part of Mesopotamia, Hammurabi published a list of 300 laws by carving them into a black basalt pillar seven feet high and two feet in diameter, which he erected near the site of the modern city of Baghdad in Iraq. Moses claimed to have received at least some of his laws directly from God while the Hebrews wandered through the Sinai desert after leaving Egypt. Nearly all the Hebrew laws are recorded in their holy book, the Torah (the Law), which makes up the first five books of the Hebrew Bible, or Old Testament.

Although both Hammurabi and Moses are famous as lawgivers, scholars are quick to point out that Hammurabi's famous "Code" was not really a modern collection of laws, nor were the laws in it particularly new. The same is true of the "laws of Moses." In both cases, the laws and traditions ascribed to these men were derived in part from earlier traditions. Hammurabi's Code is a collection of time-honored Mesopotamian legal principles developed earlier in the Sumerian cities. Many of the laws in the Mosaic, or Covenant Code of the Hebrews found in Exodus, borrow heavily from Hammurabi's code; others, especially those in Deuteronomy, were developed in the late seventh century B.C.E., long after the Hebrews had left the desert and established themselves in Palestine. Hammurabi and Moses became symbols of the traditions and values of their respective civilizations; Moses, in particular, became a nucleus around which legends formed.

It was easy for legends to form because so little was known about the lives of Hammurabi and Moses. Hammurabi was an active ruler who spent the last fourteen years of his reign in continuous warfare, attempting to control the people along the Euphrates River. He wanted "to make justice appear in the land, to destroy the evil and the wicked [so] that the strong might not oppress the weak."[1] We know the familiar story of Moses told in Exodus: how the infant was found by the Pharaoh's daughter in a basket made of bulrushes (the same story is told of an early Mesopotamian king); how the adult Moses killed an Egyptian, then fled to Midian, where he became a shepherd and the son-in-law of a Midian priest; how God called him from a burning bush to lead his people out of Egypt; and how he did this, probably during the reign of Pharaoh Rameses II (1304–1237 B.C.E.).

It is interesting that Moses is presented throughout this book as a fully human person on whom God "imposes" his will. This reflects the unique relationship between God and humankind in the Hebrew tradition. The Hebrew God was so different from humans that his image could not be drawn nor his name spoken or written in full except on special occasions, yet he made agreements with a weak and fallible people. Other ancient peoples, unlike the Hebrews, often depicted their gods in human or animal form rather than seeing humans as made in the image of God. The book of Exodus also shows Moses to be a man passionately concerned with social justice and what we call today "national liberation." No nonscriptural source of that time speaks of him, and so our knowledge of Moses is limited by what scriptures tell us about Moses as the leader, prophet, and liberator of his people.[2]

The actual lives of these men are less important than what the laws ascribed to them tell about the lifestyle of their peoples. The laws of Hammurabi as well as those in the Old Testament tell us much about what the Babylonians and Hebrews considered important; reading them allows us to look into their law courts, temples, businesses, homes, and even their hearts and minds. We can see how their values differed from ours, as well as how they were similar. In the final analysis, the laws of the Babylonians, a commercial, city-oriented people who worshipped many gods, differed significantly from those of the Hebrews, a pastoral people who worshipped a single deity called Yahweh.

Initially, however, the similarities between the laws of these two peoples are more striking than the differences. The most famous feature of Hammurabi's Code is its emphasis on the law of retaliation *(lex talionis)*. This demands, in the words of laws 196 and 200, that "if a man has put out the eye of a free man, they shall put out his eye. . . . If a man knocks out the tooth of a free man equal in rank to himself, they shall knock out his tooth." Law 209 states "If a man strikes the daughter of a free man and causes her to lose the fruit of her womb, he shall pay 10 shekels of silver." In the oldest Hebrew laws, those of the Covenant Code found in Exodus, we read: "When men strive together, and hurt a woman with child, so that there is a miscarriage . . . the one who hurt her shall be fined, according as the woman's husband shall lay upon him; and he shall pay as the judge determines. If any harm follows, then you shall give life for life, eye for eye, tooth for tooth, hand for hand, burn for burn, wound for wound, stripe for stripe."[3] In this case, the Hebrew laws seem to be a clear summary and paraphrase of the earlier Babylonian statutes.

Hebrew and Mesopotamian laws dealing with lying are also similar, the law in Hammurabi's code reading crisply: "If a man has come forward in a case to bear witness to a felony and then has not proved the statement he has made, if that case is a capital one, that man shall be put to death." In Deuteronomy 19:16–19, someone who wished to accuse another of wrongdoing has to "appear before the Lord," that is, the priests and judges, who "shall inquire diligently, and if the witness . . . has accused his brother falsely, then you shall do to him as he had meant to do to his brother. . . ." Two verses later, we find the *lex talionis* repeated again: "Your eye shall not pity; it shall be life for life, eye for eye, tooth for tooth, hand for hand, foot for foot." Hammurabi's laws and those of Moses dealing with people being placed in slavery as payment for debts are also similar, although the Hebrews required such people to serve six years in order to earn their freedom, while the Babylonians specified three. It was interesting that in both cases a man could place his wife or child in temporary servitude in payment for his debt.[4]

Rules dealing with marriage are also similar in the laws of Hammurabi and those of Moses. In both societies, controlling sexual relations was very important. This is understandable if we realize that here, as in most early societies, marriage was, first and foremost, a legal contract aimed at the production of children and the safeguarding of property rights for both parties. A Babylonian woman brought to her marriage a dowry, which was designed to protect her and her children from arbitrary action by her husband more than it was intended to enrich him. This is clear from several divorce laws which state that, in case of divorce, sanctioned if the woman were barren, the husband "shall give her money to the value of her bridal gift and shall make good to her the dowry which she brought from her father's house." Hebrew divorce law was less protective of the wife. A man could divorce his wife if he had "found some indecency in her"; he had only to "write her a bill of divorce and put it in her hand and send her out of his house."[5] In both societies, a barren woman could avoid divorce by allowing her husband to have children by a "slave-girl." This practice, followed by the Hebrew patriarch, Abraham, and described in the book of Genesis, shows the importance of child-bearing. Abraham came from this area south of Babylonia and lived several centuries before Hammurabi. Hebrew laws allowing children by slave women are similar to Hammurabi's, which derive from earlier Sumerian traditions. The importance of properly caring for children in Hammurabi's society is clear in several laws which gave a woman the right to live with another man ("enter another man's house") if her husband had left her for an extended period of time without adequate support. The husband, who might have been a prisoner of war or on a business trip that took longer than planned, did have the right to reclaim his family when he returned. However, if the woman had been amply provided for and still entered another man's house, the judge was required to "convict that woman and cast her into the water."[6]

This last provision raises the question of sexual fidelity in marriage, a problem as old as humankind and one that people in traditional societies had to deal with because important questions of inheritance were at stake. Both societies were generally harsh in punishing infidelity. "If a woman has procured the death of her husband on account of another man, they shall impale that woman," reads law 153 in Hammurabi's code. "If a man is found lying with the wife of another man, both of them shall die," according to Deuteronomy 22:22. As we might expect, each society condemned not only adultery but also homosexuality, violating "betrothed virgins," and incest. In Hammurabi's code, a man was banished for having carnal relations with his daughter and could be "cast into the water" for "lying in the bosom" of his son's fiancée. A son and his mother were burned for sleeping together after the father/husband's death. Hebrew law included long lists of persons whose "nakedness" was not to be "uncovered." The list included all members of the immediate family, as well as aunts, uncles, sisters-in-law, half-brothers and -sisters, grandchildren, and, finally, for good measure, "any beast."[7]

This prohibition against bestiality highlights a difference between Hebrew and Babylonian marriage laws. Unlike the subjects of Hammurabi, the people of Moses were concerned with more than just keeping lines of inheritance clear. In both Leviticus and Deuteronomy, there is a concern with morality and holiness, as well as with property rights. Many of the statements in Deuteronomy end with the words "so you shall purge the evil from Israel." Violations of these laws are called "defilements" in Leviticus and are considered abominable because they affect the community spiritually as well as socially; Yahweh would look unfavorably upon the Hebrew community if such individual defilements were allowed to exist unpunished.

Differences between the laws of Hammurabi and those of Moses become clearer as we look at statutes relating to agriculture. Babylonian lands were honeycombed with irrigation canals and dikes, whose upkeep was crucial to the welfare of the entire Mesopotamian area. Therefore, it is not surprising to read that, if a farmer were lax in maintaining the irrigation canals on his land, thus allowing water to break through a dike and flood a neighbor's field, he would have to replace the lost crop. If he could not afford to do this, "he and his goods" would be sold to pay the debts to his neighbor. Hammurabi's code also assumed that most land was rented out and provided very specific protections for the landlord if the rented land was not properly cultivated. Hebrew society in Palestine, by contrast, was largely pastoral with few large cities. Most land was owned by individuals and not rented out, and the people, in general, were poorer. The law of Moses, therefore, says little about landlord-tenant relationships but much about the responsibility of farmers toward the poor. Land was to lie fallow every seven years so that the poor could gather the residue from such fields, orchards, or vineyards. The Hebrews were also told not to clear their fields or vineyards entirely, but to leave a strip around the edge "for the poor and for the sojourner."[8] No such humanitarian injunctions are found in Hammurabi's code, indicating not only that Babylonian society was more centralized, urban, wealthy, and highly structured, but also that the Hebrews consciously tried to temper justice with mercy. Hammurabi's code also naturally reflects the complex, differentiated social structure of the densely populated Mesopotamian region. Slaves are one of three groups of people mentioned in the code. There were two other major classes—*awilum,* or free men, and *muskenum,* or those dependent upon another. Men in the last group were sometimes called "villeins" or "subjects." They were similar to modern sharecroppers or tenant farmers. They were clearly submissive to others, either to their upper-class landlord or to the king—since much of the land was owned directly by the government. The eyes and teeth of villeins were not worth as much as those of free men. Law 201, for example, specified that one who knocked out the tooth of a villein pay one-third maneh of silver; law 198 required that the broken bone or the eye of a villein be paid for with one maneh of silver. While this was a considerable sum (slightly over a pound of silver), it was better than losing an eye, which is what would happen to you if you put out the eye of a free man.[9]

Justice, therefore, had a clear relationship to class standing in Hammurabi's kingdom. Class differences even affected the cost of medical services. Surgery cost a free man ten shekels (2–3 ounces of silver), a villein five, and a slave only two—if the patient lived. If the patient was a free man and died during surgery, the surgeon could lose his hand; if the victim of poor surgery was only a slave, the surgeon had only to replace the man with another.[10] These penalties, class bias aside, were deliberate attempts to encourage efficiency. And, in a society where a single broken dike, bad harvest, or unprotected city wall could mean disaster, harsh measures taken to ensure efficiency were understandable.

The government's attempts to control daily life rivaled that of modern authoritarian states and the penalties for inefficiency were severe in this society,. Consider the ale-wife who would be put to death under law 109 if she failed to turn in felons who frequented her ale-house, or the builder (law 229) who knew he would be executed if a house he built fell down, killing the householder. Efficiency was important to the shipbuilder, who was forced by law to guarantee his work.[11]

The Hebrew Torah, on the other hand, has no such rules, since the semi-nomadic pastoral nomads of Palestine did not have commercial house builders or a maritime industry. Hammurabi had inscribed dozens of laws on his pillar which have no parallels in the laws of Moses: sixteen laws defining the duties of soldiers, constables, and tax collectors; eleven dealing with physicians; twelve regulating the activity of merchants (including wine sellers); six each concerning the obligations of house builders and boatmen; one dealing with the collision of ships; and over a dozen regulating wages and prices.[12]

These last—those regulating wages and prices—are detailed and famous. Wages for tailors, carpenters, potters, jewelers, blacksmiths, leather-workers, and brick-layers were all fixed by law. Modern economists frown on wage and price fixing, claiming that it stifles private initiative, encourages black market activity, or, at best, causes shortages of goods and services. While we do not know how strictly the wage and price laws in Hammurabi's code were followed, we do know that the Babylonian economy had a large amount of state control but also a strong "private sector." Since much land was owned directly by the king, many of the villeins or tenant farmers were, in effect, government employees. Yet the Babylonians developed a form of capitalism "by providing interest as an incentive for investing capital." One section of the code limits the interest rate to 20 percent on loans of grain or silver.[13] Hammurabi even wrote measures regulating conduct among business partners, merchants, and their salespeople, and grain bin owners and their customers.

We might naturally ask how such elaborate laws were enforced. Soldiers and police can try to enforce laws, whether they are fair or not, but for laws to last as long as these it is necessary for decisions of judges to be backed by some moral authority which both parties in court can respect. No pre-modern legal system works without religious sanction, and when we look at the authority behind the laws in the Babylonian and Hebrew civilizations we can better understand why the Old Testament laws had a more profound moral effect on human history than those devised by the Mesopotamians and codified by Hammurabi.

Earlier we noticed that the Hebrew laws concerning agriculture were marked by a humanitarian emphasis not found in their Babylonian counterparts. This concern for the less fortunate is clear throughout the Torah. In the earlier laws found in Exodus, the followers of Moses were told twice: "You shall not wrong a stranger or oppress him, for you were strangers in the land of Egypt." One of these passages continues: "You shall not afflict any widow or orphan. If you do afflict them, and they cry out to me, I will surely hear their cry; and my wrath will burn, and I will kill you with the sword, and your wives shall become widows and your children fatherless." Later, in Leviticus, the Hebrews are warned not to oppress their neighbors, including the deaf and the blind, and to "not be partial to the poor or defer to the great." In Deuteronomy 10:17–19, the sanction for all of these warnings becomes clear:

For the Lord your God is God of gods and Lord of lords, the great, the mighty, and the terrible God, who is not partial and takes no bribes. He executes justice for the fatherless and the widow, and loves the sojourner, giving him food and clothing. Love the sojourner therefore; for you were sojourners in the land of Egypt.[14]

From at least the time of Moses, the Hebrews believed in a single, all-powerful God, Yahweh, the "God of gods and Lord of lords." In their early history, the Hebrews accepted the fact that other people worshipped other gods; they simply believed that their god, Yahweh, was more powerful. This belief, sometimes called henotheism, evolved into full-scale monotheism, the belief that there exists only one god for everyone. But, even before Moses, the Hebrews believed that their laws, starting with the Ten Commandments and ending with a host of regulations governing the details of everyday behavior, were given to them directly by Yahweh. And, as these passages from the Torah indicate, Yahweh not only sought justice for his people; he loved them as well.

Nowhere in Hammurabi's code, for example, do we find a law telling a businessman not to charge interest when he loans money to the poor and adding: "if you take your neighbor's garment in pledge, you shall restore it to him before the sun goes down; for that is his only covering, it is his mantle . . . in what else shall he sleep?" And, as usual in the Torah, this injunction is followed by the enforcing statement: "And if he cries to me, I will hear, for I am compassionate."[15] In other places the word *compassionate* is replaced with such words as *faithful, just,* and *holy.*

Of course, Hammurabi's code, despite the modern sound of many of its provisions, was not a "secular" document. Hammurabi himself clearly believed in the existence of the gods and in a moral universe which their actions sustained—with his help. He ended his code by asking the gods to curse anyone who would change his work. He asked Ninlil, "the great mother," to destroy the land, ruin the people, and "pour out the life-blood" of any future ruler who would change the Code. Shamash, "the great judge of heaven and earth," was called upon not only to kill such a man but "to make his ghost thirst for water in the world below." Ishtar, "the lady of battle and conflict," was asked to leave the armies of anyone bold enough to change the laws "a heap of corpses on the plain."[16]

Although Hammurabi ended by calling upon the gods, his code is remembered not as a great moral document but, rather, as one of the first great legal statements of the notion that the injured should receive compensation, and harsh punishments should be used as a deterrent to crime. These Babylonian principles found their way into Hebrew law and later into other legal systems; they are found in the laws of many modern nations.

Though they did borrow heavily from the Mesopotamians, the Hebrews passed on a different legacy. While the Mosaic code is followed in detail today by only a small number of Orthodox Jews, the general moral principles of the Torah, especially the Ten Commandments and the concern for the poor and oppressed, have become an integral part of the laws and political practices of many modern nations. Just as some of our modern civil laws giving people the right to sue for personal injuries might be said to have descended from Babylonian laws, so, too, do many of our laws protecting the poor remind us of the principles of the Old Testament.

Perhaps this is why, even today, when we hear the phrase "an eye for an eye and a tooth for a tooth," we "know" it came from "the Bible." Given all the borrowing he did in putting together his code, Hammurabi would probably understand—and let us escape with only a small curse for misunderstanding the origin of the *lex talionis*.

Notes

1. G. R. Driver and John C. Miles, eds., *The Babylonian Laws*, vol. II (Oxford: Clarendon Press, 1952), 7; this complete annotated translation of Hammurabi's laws is hereafter referred to as *Laws*.

2. In addition to the many encyclopedia articles on Moses, see Andre Neher, *Men of Wisdom: Moses and the Vocation of the Jewish People*, trans. by Irene Marinoff (New York: Harper and Row, 1959); Martin Noth, *A History of Pentateuchal Traditions*, trans. and introduced by Bernhard W. Anderson (Englewood Cliffs, NJ: Prentice-Hall, 1972), 156–174; Elie Wiesel, "Moses: Portrait of a Leader," in *Messengers of God: Biblical Portraits and Legends* (New York: Random House, 1976), 174–205.

3. Driver and Miles, *Laws*, II, 78–79; Exodus 22:22–25. All citations from the Old Testament are taken from *The Oxford Annotated Bible*, Revised Standard Version (New York: Oxford University Press, 1962).

4. Driver and Miles, *Laws*, II, 15, 48–49; Deuteronomy 19:16–19; Deut. 15:12–18; Exod. 21:2–11.
5. Driver and Miles, *Laws*, II, 55; Deuteronomy 24:1.
6. Driver and Miles, *Laws*, II, 53–57; Being "cast into the water" in Hammurabi's code refers to a trial in which a defendant would be bound and thrown into the river: if he or she floated, he or she was deemed innocent; if the person sank, he or she was considered guilty—as well as dead, verdict and sentence being determined nearly simultaneously.
7. Driver and Miles, *Laws*, II, 57, 61; Leviticus 18:6–23. The differences between Hammurabi's code and Hebrew laws dealing with chastity, marriage, and divorce are also summarized in George Barton, *Archeology and the Bible* (Philadelphia: American Sunday School Union, 1916), 326–329.
8. Driver and Miles, *Laws*, II, 27–31; Exod. 23:10–11, Leviticus 19:9, Deuteronomy 24:19–22.
9. Driver and Miles, *Laws*, II, 77.
10. Ibid., 79, 81.
11. Ibid., 45, 83, 85.
12. Ibid., 21–27, 79–81, 43–45, 83–85, 89–93; see also Barton, *Archeology and the Bible*, 316–317, 322, 336–339.
13. Cyrus H. Gordon, editor, *Hammurabi's Code: Quaint or Forward-Looking?* (New York: Holt, Rinehart and Winston, 1957), 8.
14. Exodus 22:21–27; 23:9; Leviticus 19:13–15; Deuteronomy 10:17–19.
15. Exodus 22:25–27.
16. Driver and Miles, *Laws*, II, 95–107.

Further Reading

BARTON, GEORGE. *Archeology and the Bible.* Philadelphia: American Sunday School Union, 1916. Old but includes wonderfully succinct comparisons.

GAAD, CYRIL. "Hammurabi: The End of His Dynasty," in *Cambridge Ancient History.* 3d ed. Vol. II. Cambridge: Cambridge Press, 1975. Good, short account of the man.

GORDON, CYRUS H., ed. *Hammurabi's Code: Quaint or Forward-Looking?* New York: Holt, Rinehart and Winston, 1957. Scholars debate the role and value of the Code.

NEHER, ANDRE. *Men of Wisdom: Moses and the Vocation of the Jewish People.* Trans. by Irene Marinoff. New York: Harper and Row, 1959. Insight into the man and his mission.

CHAPTER 2

Zoroaster and Buddha: Explaining Suffering

Why does evil exist in the world? The "Western" Zoroaster and the "Eastern" Buddha answer this question quite differently. What are some implications of their answers for our understanding of world history?

Why do people suffer? Why does evil exist in the world? These questions, asked by millions of people throughout human history, have helped inspire most of humanity's great philosophies and religions. While the questions are simple, the answers which thinkers have given to them are often complicated—and certainly varied.

During the sixth century before the birth of Christ, several important attempts were made to explain suffering and evil. Chinese sage Kung Fuzi (Confucius, 551–479 B.C.E.) believed that suffering was caused by people's failure to love and respect one another properly. The system of ethics he devised to remedy this lack of mutual respect helped mold Chinese civilization for over two thousand years. In this same, very creative period, other men offered religious answers to the problem of suffering. Two notable seekers of truth were Zarathustra (ca. 628–551 B.C.E.), a Persian nobleman and founder of a religion known as Zoroastrianism, and Siddhartha Gautama (ca. 560–480 B.C.E.), an Indian known later as the Buddha and founder of Buddhism. These two men offered specific and very different answers to our questions about suffering and evil. Their ideas also deserve our attention because their respective philosophies represent two ways of looking at the world—one of which can be called "Western" and the other "Eastern."

It may seem unusual to refer to Zarathustra, or Zoroaster (the Greek version of his name, by which he is usually known), as a Westerner, since he was born not far from the modern Iranian capital of

15

Teheran in what many today call the Middle East or Western Asia. Yet, in Zoroaster's day, the Greek cities were on the Western fringe of the civilized world and the Persian Empire itself was considered the East by those in the Mediterranean world. Zoroaster was probably a priest and a member of the Spitama clan in Persia. His early life was apparently ordinary, but about age twenty he left home (which may have included his three wives and six children) and began to wander the countryside, seeking Truth. After ten years of wandering, he had a vision of an angel, Vohu Manah (Good Thought), who told Zoroaster that there was only one God, Ahura Mazda (the Wise Lord), and that Zoroaster was to become his prophet. During the next several years, Zoroaster had other visions in which other messengers of Ahura Mazda appeared to him to reveal God's message. The newly anointed prophet began to preach immediately, and he was persecuted and ignored for ten years. Finally, he converted his cousin Maidhyomah to his new faith. They then journeyed East to Bactria [modern Afghanistan], where Zoroaster won over King Vishtaspa and his court. From that point, Zoroastrianism spread more rapidly among the Aryan peoples in the Persian Empire. At times the new religion was spread by war, and it was during one of these wars, we are told, that the seventy-seven-year-old Zoroaster was killed while tending the sacred fire at an altar.

It is hard to know all of Zoroaster's teachings with certainty. Many early writings were lost and his doctrines were greatly changed in later centuries, but a series of hymns, or "Gathas," generally thought to be the work of the prophet himself, suggest that this man was one of history's first monotheists.[1] While most people at this time believed that there were many gods, Zoroaster declared firmly that Ahura Mazda was the only one. He credited this God with creating the world and all the good things in it; Ahura Mazda wished all to live a life of "pure thought, pure words, and pure deeds," and he judged men after their death on how well they had succeeded.[2] Those who followed Truth during their lives would go to Heaven, while those who followed the Lie would be sent to Hell.

The existence of a Hell in Zoroaster's religion tells us, in the words of one scholar, that "although Ahura Mazda is supreme, he is not unopposed." In Zoroastrianism, the Good Spirit, or Spenta Mainyu, analogous to the Holy Spirit in Christianity, is opposed to the Bad Spirit, or Angra Mainyu. This evil spirit is very much like

Satan in traditional Christian theology; he is a "prince of darkness," the very embodiment of lies, cowardice, and all other forms of misery. Ahura Mazda allows people to choose between himself and Angra Mainyu.[3] By their free choice, men and women can both save themselves and advance the cause of goodness and truth in the world. In the final analysis, the world would be saved; Ahura Mazda would win a last great victory over the Evil Spirit—even Hell would finally come to an end.[4] Humans could bring this final judgment day closer by living a life of goodness and purity and by deeds which spread the goodness of Ahura Mazda in the world in which they lived. The moral life involved struggle and choice— here rather than in the hereafter.

If all this sounds much like the world view preached by Christianity, as well as by Judaism and Islam, for that matter, you should note that many scholars see important connections among these four Western religions. Some believe that the Jews adopted some basic ideas about good and evil, Heaven, Hell, and final judgment from the disciples of Zoroaster while the Judeans were held captive in Babylon during the sixth century (586–539 B.C.E.). These new beliefs were then inherited by Christians and Muslims, both of whom accept basic Hebrew beliefs contained in the Old Testament, or Jewish Bible. This explanation of the Zoroastrian origins of basic Western religious ideas is convenient. Unfortunately, there is no direct evidence that it is true.[5] While similarities clearly exist in the way Zoroaster and the major Western religions explain evil, no one is able to say exactly who took what from whom—or when this happened.

What we can say is that Zoroaster's explanation of evil and suffering, however it may have been modified by his own Persian followers and however it may have been adapted, or even influenced, by the Jews, has had a powerful impact on Western thought. All major Western religions since Zoroaster's day have highly valued four things: (1) the role of the individual person; (2) the material world in which we live; (3) time and human history; (4) the role of a supremely powerful, transcendent Creator God. All four were important in Zoroaster's fight against evil and suffering. Let us briefly examine each in turn.

For Zoroaster, individuals were more than helpless victims of suffering. While he believed in few rituals (veneration of fire as a symbol of truth and of water as a symbol of purity were central ones), Zoroaster did assert that good deeds would be rewarded, and he called upon his followers to be aggressive in resisting evil. One of the most prominent good deeds mentioned in the Gathas is concern for cattle. The Bactrians, people whom Zoroaster converted, were a pastoral people who survived on simple forms of agriculture and on cattle-rearing; their enemies were nomadic warriors from the north, who often invaded their settlements. Thus, it is not surprising that Zoroaster called these tribal horsemen the "followers of the Lie" and declared virtuous any action that promoted agriculture, made the earth more fruitful, or protected sheep or cattle. Good deeds might be simple deeds for sixth-century rural Persians, but virtuous human actions were important to the salvation of the world.

Since human actions were essential for the defeat of evil, the material world where such actions take place was also important. Zoroastrianism, like Judaism, Christianity, and Islam after it, was a world-affirming religion. The battle between Good and Evil was fought on earth, in the human soul but also in the home, field, or shop. Zoroaster did not believe in torturing the flesh, or in other forms of monastic self-denial. His followers were not supposed to escape from the world in order to bring themselves closer to Ahura Mazda; they were to help Ahura Mazda by living a life of virtue *in* the world.

Given this affirmation of humanity and the world, it is logical that Zoroaster would regard measurement of time as important. Although Zoroastrians do not see God intervening in human history in the ways described in the Old Testament, they do believe that the world and time itself will end with the last judgment, or the Final Rehabilitation, as some Zoroastrian scriptures refer to it.[6] In the distant but foreseeable future, the power of the Evil Spirit over humanity will be ended.

This will happen because of the ultimate power and beneficence of an all-powerful God. However important the ethical choices we must make, Ahura Mazda will have the last word: "In immortality (or eternity) shall the soul of the righteous be joyful, in perpetuity shall be the torments of the Liar. . . . Thine, Mazda, is the Dominion, whereby thou canst give to the right-living poor man the better portion."[7]

In summary, then, evil for Zoroaster was not caused by the omnipotent Supreme Being, but only permitted by him. The Spirit of Evil was a necessary consequence of free choice. If people were to be free, they had to be free to choose evil. But, if people could choose evil, they could also choose good. Suffering was caused by Angra Mainyu, aided by his followers on earth; it was painful but temporary. This explanation has at least two logical flaws: it does not explain why innocent people suffer, nor does it tell us why an all-powerful, good God would give evil such free rein in the first place. These logical flaws have been the subject of intense debate by religious philosophers through the centuries. Judged by the general directness and practical tone of Zoroaster's words in the Gathas, he was not much interested in such metaphysical abstractions. In that respect, at least, he was much like his Indian contemporary Siddhartha Gautama, who otherwise lived in a very different thought-world. Gautama's value for us is that he tried to answer just those two questions that Zoroaster left unanswered.

Like Zoroaster, Siddhartha Gautama came from the upper class. His father was ruler of a small state in northeastern India (now Nepal). Gautama's status as a nobleman was important in helping explain why he became interested in the problem of suffering. Although there are many legends about the birth and early life of this young prince, the most frequently repeated one tells us that Siddhartha's father was warned by a Hindu priest that the young man would become a famous religious leader instead of a ruler if he ever became acquainted with old age, illness, death, or the ways of a begging monk. Not wanting this to happen, Siddhartha's father tried to shield him from such things by providing him with a life of luxury. The young prince was married at sixteen and lived in a beautiful palace surrounded by young, beautiful people. One day, so we are told, Siddhartha had to leave the palace grounds and, despite his father's precautions, happened to see an old man. He asked his driver what sort of creature this was and was shocked when the driver explained old age. On three other journeys, he saw an ill person, a corpse, and a wandering monk.

After seeing these things, the sensitive prince determined to leave his fine home, his young wife, and his infant son. For six years, beginning at about age thirty, Gautama wandered through India, attempting to discover truth and tranquility by living the life of an ascetic, one who denies oneself the pleasures of the flesh, especially eating, in order to better concentrate the mind. After years of severe fasting—one legend has it that the soon-to-be Buddha ate as little as one grain of rice a day for a time—Gautama was no closer to the knowledge he sought. Finally, he stopped fasting and sat down under a tree on the banks of a river, vowing to remain there until he understood truth. In the course of one night, according to an early Buddhist scripture, Gautama achieved Enlightenment, a state of mind and soul in which he understood the nature of good and evil and was freed from the temptations and illusions that beset other men.

After this awakening, the Buddha, a term that means awakened or Enlightened one, went into the nearest town (modern Benares) and preached his first sermon in a deer park to a handful of his former companions, who had left him earlier when he stopped fasting. This Deer Park Sermon sums up the essential message of the Buddha as described in the Four Noble Truths: all existence is suffering; all suffering is caused by craving or desire; suffering can be ended by eliminating desire; and the way to end suffering is to follow the Noble Eightfold Path. The steps on this path include right views, right intentions, right speech, right action, right livelihood, right effort, right mindfulness, and right meditation. Travelers on this path follow a standard moral code which forbids lying, stealing, killing, and other forms of violence and combine this with an emphasis on meditation designed to help the individual gain "panna," or wisdom.

What was this wisdom that the Buddha preached throughout northern India until his death forty-five years after his Enlightenment? Although Buddhism has become a major world religion in Asia in the twenty-five centuries since Buddha's death, it is important to distinguish—just as it was in the case of Zoroaster—the original teachings of Gautama from those of his followers, many of whom tried to turn him into a god, the Lord Buddha. This is not something Gautama would have appreciated, for it was a fundamental conviction of his that humans, and not any divine power, were responsible for evil. Buddha did not speak of God or sin. Evil came simply from people's desires for things they could not obtain. God or gods do not punish us; we punish ourselves by our own greed and craving. Because of this very human explanation of evil, the Buddha has been called an atheist by some: for example, by a main character in Gore Vidal's novel *Creation*.[8] Although Buddha may not have been religious in the sense in which most of us understand this term, he did share a goal with Zoroaster and other religious teachers—the overcoming of death. The way he proposed we do this reveals his debt to Hinduism, as well as the basic difference between his philosophy and that of Zoroaster.

All Hindus believe in reincarnation. The individual soul is reborn, or reincarnated, many times before it reaches release (moksha), or salvation. Good actions cause one to be reborn higher in the social, or caste, system; bad actions cause one to be reborn in a lower social caste, or perhaps even as an animal. This happened according to law, not grace: one's deeds (karma) advanced or retarded one's attempt to escape from the wheel, or circle, of life. The goal of Hinduism is to eliminate death by stopping rebirth. Emancipation comes for the individual when his or her soul is merged into the world-soul (Brahman) and is no longer reborn. Buddha accepted this basic teaching. His philosophy differed from that of classical Hinduism by making salvation (which he called Nirvana) accessible to all, not just to members of the higher castes of priests, warriors, and merchants. He also espoused a "middle way" between extreme physical self-denial and excessive attachment to the world.

Buddha's "middle way" is really one of great psychological sophistication—if we accept his suppositions. If we believe with him that the physical, material world is really one of illusion (maya) and that everything that exists is impermanent, it makes sense for us to stop craving or desiring material things. But Buddha went even further. He said that the individual soul, or self, was also impermanent. Therefore, to reach Nirvana and end all suffering, one had to "extinguish" the individual ego, or self. One student of Buddhism explains this mystifying process by which an individual self is "extinguished" and enters Nirvana as follows:

> Imagine an illimitable ocean in which there are innumerable vials [bottles]. Each vial is filled with sea-water belonging to that very ocean and each is composed of a substance that gradually thickens or dissolves in response to circumstances. Under suitable conditions, it dissolves altogether, whereupon the water it contains becomes indistinguishable from the rest of the ocean. Not one drop of water ceases to exist; all that is lost is its apparent separateness. In this analogy, the water in each vial represents a so-called individual being and the gradual thickening or dissolving vial symbolizes his mental and physical characteristics . . . [which are] born of Avidya (greed) and nourished by the force of karma. . . . Once [these] have been dissolved, the being's "separate" identity ceases.[9]

How different all this was from the teachings of Zoroaster! Buddha believed struggle of any kind was part of the problem; man had to "let go" of attachments to all things and all ideas (even to the idea of nonattachment) in order to be Enlightened. The Persian prophet, on the other hand, saw struggle—as long as it was against the Evil One—as a positive good. Buddha, like many of his Hindu predecessors, saw the material world as a place to escape from; for Zoroaster it was a place where the salvation of each individual had to be worked out by life-enriching, world-blessing deeds. The single biggest difference between these two seers was the way they understood time. Zoroastrians had but one chance to achieve Heaven and avoid Hell; Buddhists could take many lifetimes to reach Nirvana. Zoroaster, like all Western religious leaders, saw time as finite. Humanity and the world would end, either sooner or later, but at some foreseeable point. Buddhists and Hindus saw time as virtually endless; for them the universe was created and recreated over vast periods of time known to Buddhists as kalpas. When someone asked Buddha how long a kalpa was, he asked the questioner to imagine a man wiping a mighty mountain peak once each century with a handkerchief. That mountain would be worn away before a kalpa had passed.[10]

We can imagine these two famous teachers engaging in a debate. Buddha would smile tranquilly while pointing out to Zoroaster that his God, Ahura Mazda, was playfully cruel in giving people only one chance at salvation. Zoroaster, who disliked paradoxes as much as Buddha enjoyed them, would sternly charge the Buddha with being just plain silly in denying the reality of the material world. The two would agree only that men and women ought to live a good life, and avoid evil in order to achieve salvation. On how to do this, there would be fundamental, dare we say eternal, disagreement.

Of course, a debate such as this could never have taken place, even if the Buddha had lived closer to Zoroaster and had not been nine years old when the Persian leader died. Debating itself is a Western device; it assumes that Truth can be discovered through rational discourse. Buddha would have found debating itself useless, for he believed that ultimate Truth could be discovered only through what we call intuition and meditation. Metaphysical speculation and rational argument were of little value to him.

Much of the history of what we call Eastern civilizations makes more sense to us if we understand the values of the Buddha and his followers. The lack of emphasis that many Eastern countries have historically placed on material progress, for example, makes greater sense if we understand Buddhism. The fact that Western nations were the first to pursue material progress and industrialization aggressively also follows logically from the world-view of Zoroaster. If you find, however, on finishing this essay, that the tenets of Zoroaster make more sense to you than do those of the Buddha . . . but if at the same time you are intrigued, even strangely attracted, by the psycho-logic of Buddha's view of the way to eliminate evil, be thankful! Living in the interdependent world of today, you have more paths to Truth open to you than could be found in the wildest dreams of either Zoroaster or Buddha.

Notes

1. The fourteenth-century (B.C.E.) Egyptian Pharaoh Akhenaten and the thirteenth-century Hebrew leader Moses are both examples of monotheists before Zoroaster.

2. Rustom Masani, *Zoroastrianism: The Religion of the Good Life* (New York: Macmillan, 1968), 8.

3. John Noss, *Man's Religions*, 6th ed. (New York: Macmillan, 1980), 336–339. Because of the importance of the Evil Spirit in Zoroaster's teaching, some scholars believe that his religion was really dualistic instead of monotheistic, that he believed in two gods of equal power, one good and the other evil. The more common opinion, however, is that Zoroaster himself believed in one Supreme Being, but that Persian priests (Magi) centuries after his death made the religion dualistic by stressing the power of Angra Mainyu (called Ahriman in later Zoroastrian writings). For more on this, see James W. Boyd and Donald A. Crosby, "Is Zoroastrianism Dualistic or Monotheistic?" *Journal of the American Academy of Religion,* 47 (1979): 557–588; Mary Boyce, *A History of Zoroastrianism,* vol. I (Leiden: E. J. Brill, 1975), 193–196.

4. R. C. Zaehner, *The Dawn and Twilight of Zoroastrianism* (New York: G. P. Putnam's, 1961), 302–321; Boyce, *History,* 233.

5. For contrasting views on the connection between Zoroastrianism and Judaism, see R. C. Zaehner, "Zoroastrianism," in *The Concise Encyclopedia of Living Faiths,* ed. R. C. Zaehner, (Boston: Beacon, 1959), 222; Masani, *Zoroastrianism,* 18–25; James H. Moulton, *Early Zoroastrianism: The Origins, the Prophet, the Magi* (Amsterdam: Philo Press, 1872), 288–291, 300–301, 321–322; Boyce, *History,* 246.

6. Zaehner, *Dawn and Twilight of Zoroastrianism,* 308–311.

7. See the hymns or Gathas (Yasna 45 and Yasna 53), quoted in Moulton, *Early Zoroastrianism*, 371, 389–390.
8. Gore Vidal, *Creation* (New York: Ballantine Books, 1982), 276–277.
9. John Blofeld, *The Tantric Mysticism of Tibet* (New York: E. P. Dutton, 1970), 58–59.
10. Kenneth K. S. Ch'en, *Buddhism: The Light of Asia* (Woodbury, NY: Barrons Educational Series, 1968), 42.

Further Reading

HESSE, HERMANN. *Siddhartha*. New York: Bantam Books, 1971. A fictionalized biography of the Buddha which captures the spirit of his message in a form attractive to modern Westerners.

VIDAL, GORE. *Creation*. New York: Ballantine Books, 1982. Well-written, if lengthy, historical novel, starring Zoroaster's grandson, which discusses the great ideas of the creative sixth century before Christ.

WATTS, ALAN. *The Way of Zen*. New York: Pantheon Books, 1957. A clear, short, and provocative interpretation of Buddhist ideas for Westerners.

ZAEHNER, R. C. *The Teachings of the Magi: A Compendium of Zoroastrian Beliefs*. New York: Oxford University Press, 1976. After the various encyclopedias, Zaehner's works are the best on this subject.

CHAPTER 3

Confucius and Plato:
A Few Really Good People

What is the best way to create a strong society? Can people be led by moral example because they are basically good—or do they need a philosopher-king to help them control the evil within themselves?

What is the best way to create a strong society? History offers many answers. Hammurabi of Babylon, as we saw, believed in harsh laws, while Jesus of Nazareth saw love as the key. Most of us have ideas that fall somewhere in between. Given the many different answers to this basic question, it is striking how similar were many ideas of the ancient Chinese sage Confucius (Kung Fuzi or "Master Kung," 551–479 B.C.E.) and famous Greek philosopher Plato (427–347 B.C.E.). Both believed that a good society or state had to be led by men of superior virtue and wisdom. Both generally distrusted laws because they made people devious and merchants because they fostered greed. Neither favored democratic self-government, but both believed in the existence of absolute moral truth and in the possibility that humans could live in peace and harmony. Both focused attention on the individual, but neither believed in "individual rights" in the way we use that phrase, but rather stressed individual duty.

Before we explain these similarities by saying that "great minds think alike," we should note several important differences between these two philosophers. While both believed that only those who were already virtuous could create a well-ordered, peaceful political community or state, Confucius and his followers were convinced that all human beings were basically good, or could be nurtured to be so. Plato begged to differ; he thought most people were far too easily deceived by tyrants or greed. They needed to be controlled, either by their carefully educated "betters" or by laws.

Naturally, these differing views of human nature resulted in different versions of the ideal government. Confucius emphasized human behavior in general, while Plato stressed the importance of the behavior of a carefully educated ruling class. While Confucius was more interested in the relationship of individuals within a community, Plato was more interested in universal truths. Both believed that *education* was necessary to produce a wise ruling class—but Confucius believed education could do this in and of itself while Plato's system almost creates a closed ruling *caste* of leaders. This is something worth noting since caste is usually associated with the "East," "democracy" (broadly defined) with the "West." Their views have been widely studied and have affected the lives of millions over the centuries. Yet their insights, however universal in nature, also reflect the unique features of their respective civilizations.

Confucius was the son of a minor nobleman during the "Period of Warring States" in ancient Chinese history. From about 1050 to 770 B.C.E., the Zhou emperors held together the various Chinese states using a feudal system of government in which loyalty to the rulers was based on marriage alliances and other personal contracts between them and various noble families. This delicate system of mutual dependence and harmony had collapsed by Confucius' day, and he took it as his mission to show people how it—and political unity—could be restored. Confucius married at age nineteen and had three children, but "his relations with his wife and children were without cordiality."[1] As a young man, Confucius took a minor administrative position with a noble family in his home state of Lu and later worked intermittently for the ruler of Lu as a minister, taking fifteen years off to study the history of the Zhou rulers and educate himself in the noble arts of ritual, music, archery, charioteering, arithmetic, and calligraphy [art of drawing characters used in Chinese writing]. When Confucius realized that the ruler of Lu was more interested in dancing girls that in the serious business of governing, he resigned and spent the rest of his life as a teacher, trying unsuccessfully to find another ruler who would appreciate his advice. He died at the age of seventy-three, after transmitting to many students the message that China could be strong again if the values and virtues of the past were restored. During the next two generations, his disciples compiled his teachings in a book known as the *Analects* ("Sayings"). "No book," wrote a recent translator, "in the entire history of the world has exerted, over a longer period of time, a greater influence on a large number of people than this slim little volume."[2] Other Confucian ideas are contained in works written by his students and followers, including *The Doctrine of the Mean, The Great Learning*, and *Mencius* [the name of one of his disciples].

Hardly the stuffy or severe person often depicted in legend, Confucius was physically strong and a good hunter and sportsman, who spent much of his life traveling at a time when this required considerable stamina. He taught his followers that civilization depended on virtue, and especially on the virtues of "humanity" (*ren*, translated as "human-heartedness," "love," or "benevolence") and "propriety" or "correct behavior" (*li*). In its simplest form, *ren* means to treat others with humaneness and respect, as you would like to be treated. (There are three statements of the Golden Rule in the *Analects*.[3]) A person with *ren* would show his or her respect for others by proper behavior or civility. *Li* is not mindless bowing to others but a whole set of customs that brings order to our lives and helps us show our love for our fellow humans. The formal aspects of Confucian etiquette are important ways to convey our attitudes. "Authority without generosity, ceremony without reverence, mourning without grief—these I cannot bear to contemplate," Confucius said.[4] A good society would exist if people were honest with themselves and caring toward each other.

While Confucius believed that all could develop through education the virtues of *ren* and *li*, he generally described these as the qualities of a "gentleman." Although Confucius understood that most leaders of society would be aristocrats, he did not believe that only the members of the upper classes were, or could be, virtuous. With the proper education, anyone—providing he was male—could develop the wisdom of a true leader or sage. One became a "gentleman" by education in history and literature, not by birth, and the true leader, whatever his background, should lead by moral example. To influence people, "approach them with dignity and they will be respectful. Be yourself a good son and kind father, and they will be loyal." He believed that "when their betters cultivate civility [*ren*], the people are easily led."[5]

It is clear that Confucius envisioned a society in which human relationships—especially those within the family—were more important than laws. Any summary of the ideas of Confucius will mention the importance of the duties of children toward their parents and family. It will also mention the importance of the Five

Relationships described in the *Doctrine of the Mean*, those between ruler and subject, father and son, husband and wife, older and younger brother, and friends.[6] If all involved in these relationships behaved properly and with full human respect toward the other party, society would be orderly. An orderly society is a well-governed one, but here the knowledge, sincerity, and wisdom of the ruler was as important as his behavior. This is made clear in a passage from *The Great Learning*, which points out that ancient rulers, wishing to "order well" their states, had to first "regulate" their families. This required that they "first cultivate their personal lives." They did this by being sincere and trying to extend their knowledge through "the investigation of things." Once "things were investigated," their "knowledge was extended," their wills were made sincere, and their personal lives were improved. This led to the proper regulation of their families and "when the family [was properly] regulated, the state [was] in order and there [was] peace in the world.[7] The Chinese believed there was a moral order in the universe. A good leader, reflecting this moral order by living a just and proper life himself, would more easily win the trust of his subjects. If his life were balanced and harmonious, there would be harmony in the country. All this did not mean that a good ruler could ignore the crops or disband the army; it simply meant that these things were not enough—the successful ruler also had to set a moral example that others were able to imitate. Confucius' follower Mencius put it bluntly in his advice to a ruler who asked him how to govern:

> You'd better get back to basics. If mulberry trees are planted on plots of one acre, people in their fifties can wear silk. If you do not pull men away for battle during the breeding times of your livestock, people in their seventies can eat meat. . . . Pay careful attention to education, teaching the Justice of filial piety and fraternity, and the grey-haired will not be seen in the streets carrying heavy burdens on their backs.[8]

The emphasis by Confucius on the importance of human relationships became popular in part because Chinese society already put much emphasis on the family. Early Chinese religion, like that in many other early human societies, involved intense respect for and veneration of one's ancestors. Within three centuries of his death, Confucius' ideas, modified to stress the importance of loyal subjects and to deemphasize such things as the moral duty of intellectuals to criticize unjust rulers,[9] had become the ruling philosophy of the Han dynasty. And the moral gentlemen of Confucians became the bureaucrats of the Chinese state for the next sixteen centuries. Bureaucrats tend to value rules for their own sake, and this is why many people—in China and elsewhere—came to associate *li* with ritual for its own sake, instead of seeing it as a manifestation of *ren*. After several centuries of what came to be called State Confucianism, no "gentlemen" would speak as bluntly to a ruler as Mencius had done. When the ideas of creative thinkers become the official policy of a government, they become more influential because they are backed by state power. However, they can also lose some of their original "edge." This happened to the ideas of Confucius over the centuries as millions memorized his words to pass state civil service examinations but far fewer tried to live them in the way he must have intended.

Whether Plato's ideas on government have been misinterpreted in the centuries since his death is harder to determine, if only because everything written by this "father of Western philosophy" has been the subject of extensive discussion and debate. Plato's political and ethical ideas seem more complex than those of Confucius, at least to those of us with a modern Western education and biases. Yet Plato's understanding of human nature, and consequently of the ideal state, were as influenced by the events in fifth century Athens as Confucius' ideas were by the disorder of the Warring States period in China.

Like Confucius, Plato was born into an aristocratic family. His father claimed descent from the last of the kings of Athens and his mother was related to sixth-century leader Solon, who established some of the first democratic institutions in the city. Plato grew up during the Peloponnesian War,[10] which saw the Athenians replace their democratic government with an oligarchic [rule by a group] one known as the "Thirty Tyrants." These were in turn overthrown by democratic forces after Athens lost the war to Sparta. This democratic government, however, fearful of internal enemies after Athens' defeat, put Plato's teacher, Socrates, to death in 399 B.C.E. for "corrupting the youth," that is, asking too many questions. Both by family background and by virtue of his experiences as a young man, Plato was familiar with different types of government. Growing up in such a troubled time, it is perhaps not surprising that he devoted much of his life—and a major book, the *Republic*—to trying to determine the best form of government.

Also like his Chinese counterpart, Plato spent time traveling but most of his life teaching. While in his twenties, he traveled to Egypt, Italy, and Sicily. In two visits to the city of Syracuse in Sicily in the 360s, Plato tried unsuccessfully to tutor the ruler, Dionysus II, in hopes that he would become the ideal "philosopher-king" Plato described in the *Republic*. Plato had already purchased land near Athens and established a school, the Academy, where he taught young men his principles of ethics and government, "to educate citizens for statesmanship." This school, which some call the first university, remained in existence for nearly 900 years.[11] During his long life, Plato wrote many philosophical dialogues, lengthy written conversations in which Plato's ideas on the nature of morality, truth, beauty, and justice are put in the mouth of his teacher, Socrates. The *Republic,* one of the longest dialogues, contains Plato's picture of the ideal state and of the virtues and education of the people who were to govern it, led by a philosopher-king.

Before we can understand why Plato thought that philosophers—literally "lovers of wisdom"—made the best rulers, we need to appreciate his belief that society or the state should be organized to reflect our basic human nature. In the first place, like most thoughtful Greeks of this period, Plato believed that only in the city-state, or *polis,* could a human being find fulfillment. Second, Plato believed that each human soul consisted of three parts, a rational part, a part containing our desires or appetites for pleasure and wealth, and a part he called the spirited part, which contained a person's love of honor and desire for victory. Each part of the soul then corresponded to one of the three social classes in Plato's political community. The spirited part was best represented by the military class, or soldiers. The general population of "producers," or craftsmen and merchants, represented the desires or appetites, and the rational part of the soul was most active in the ruling class of "guardians." In a harmonious state, just as in a harmonious individual, all of the parts must work together. For this to happen in a well-governed state, the rational part must control the other two.[12]

In their wisdom, Plato's guardians resembled the group that Confucius called gentlemen. Yet they are different from the ruling class in China in at least one important respect. They understand ultimate or universal Truth (the idea of the Good) in a way that others cannot, even if the others are educated. To make this point, Plato wrote an allegory [a story in which the images or facts symbolize something else] of a cave. In the *Republic*, Plato asks us to imagine a cave in which prisoners are chained, from the neck down, against a wall facing the rear of the cave. Behind them is a fire and between the fire and the prisoners is a path along which the guards walk back and forth, carrying cutouts of animals and people; some guards are talking as they do this. The prisoners, who have been chained there from birth, see the shadows which the figures cast on the rear wall and mistake this for reality. If one of the prisoners was freed and dragged (since he would be afraid of the unknown) to the mouth of the cave, he would see the sun, something more "real" than the fire because it is the source of the fire. If that same prisoner, once he adjusted to the light and overcame his bewilderment, were sent back into the cave to tell the other prisoners that they were mistaking shadows for reality, they would not believe him; in fact, says Plato, they would probably try to kill him for telling such tall tales, disrupting their lives and challenging their accustomed beliefs.[13]

In this allegory, the images on the rear wall of the cave represent what most humans take to be truth or reality: talking, moving shadows. The sun represents ultimate Truth or the ultimate Good, the source of all lesser "truths." In Plato's ideal state, the ruling class of guardians, led by a philosopher-king, would govern because they were the only ones who had seen the sun or, as Plato put it, they "had knowledge" while others "had beliefs." Their natures, in which the rational part of the soul dominated, meant that they were "made to practice philosophy and be political leaders, while others shouldn't engage in philosophy and should follow a leader."[14] The guardian class was also put in control of the state in Plato's *Republic* because they had a specialized education and social life which prepared them for their leadership role. Plato's instructions for the education of his guardians goes far beyond anything that Confucius had in mind for his gentlemen.

Members of Plato's guardian class had to be reliable, courageous, and good-looking (since this was a reflection of inner worth). They would be raised in an environment in which women were equal to men, even to the point of fighting on the battlefield when necessary, and exercising naked together in the gymnasia. Men and women would share wives, husbands, and property, but guardians could mate only with other members of their class. That way, only "outstanding" children would be produced. Otherwise,

Plato wrote, "our breed of guardians will become tainted."[15] It was also permissible for members of the guardian class to tell "helpful lies" to the lesser members of the community if this was necessary "for the good of the community," for example, to get people to fight foreigners. The education of guardians would focus on physical training and on the liberal and fine arts, including music and math. They were to avoid literature, drama, and poetry which contained fantasies. Guardians had to be trained in dialectic [philosophical argument] and had to learn that the five senses were unreliable, and that all real truth was universal in nature and, thus, beyond the senses.[16] The lifestyle and education of this group was justified if we understand that rulers really were different from other people. As Plato put it,

> God included gold in the mixture when he was forming Those of you who have what it takes to be rulers (which is why rulers have the greatest privileges), silver when he was forming the auxiliaries [common soldiers, merchants, etc.], and iron and copper when he was forming the farmers and other workers.[17]

Plato's specifications for his guardians left him open to later charges, especially by twentieth-century authors, that he was elitist to the point of being totalitarian. It was almost as if he were advocating a closed caste system in contrast to the more open or "democratic" system of Confucius, in which anyone could become a "gentleman." Some have even said that the ideas in the *Republic* foreshadowed the practices of Hitler's Germany.[18] Those who try to defend him against these charges point out that Plato's rulers were hardly like modern dictators. Since they *really did know Truth and Justice*, philosopher-kings would behave justly. It has not been an altogether convincing defense. On the other hand, we should remember that Plato was describing an ideal, or utopian, state and was doing this as a way of highlighting for his readers the importance of reason. It is also true that Plato did modify some of his views later in life, when he wrote the *Statesman* and the *Laws*. In these works, he decided that the views in the *Republic* were too utopian. In the *Laws*, he suggested that it was better for people to rely on laws than on the moral leadership of a guardian class. The philosopher-king became a legislator who enforced numerous rules governing in detail the lives of citizens. It was a "second-best" solution for him, but, by that time, he was less interested in helping the select few acquire ultimate knowledge and more interested in molding the character of all citizens of the state.[19]

The fact that the views of each of these ancient thinkers have been both disputed and misunderstood by later ages—in more ways than we can discuss here—is itself a tribute to their profound impact on succeeding generations. Whatever else we might say about them, they did raise a standard of human perfectibility for their respective societies, and they did so by challenging the "commonsense" notion that things had to be the way they always had been—or had appeared to be. Each argued that life could be better, both more reasonable and more moral, if we trusted our senses less (Plato) and really believed in the human capacity for love (Confucius). There was a significant difference, however, in how human improvement was to be achieved. Confucius had faith that all men and women could behave humanely toward each other, and he believed that, if they did this, the society they would create through their ritual acts of propriety toward each other would ennoble all within it. Led by the gentlemen of knowledge and virtue, the Chinese could create a society that, if not perfect, was at least in harmony with the forces that governed the universe.

Plato had less faith than Confucius in humans' ability to create a perfect society. After all, most people in any community, he believed, were destined to live their lives mistaking shadows for reality. People were certainly able to use their reason to control their desires but they were not, as a rule, willing to do so. Therefore, in the *Republic* at least, he proposed that the only way a society could approach anything like perfection would be by giving power to the few who were able to use reason, leave the cave, and understand the Ultimate Good.

Perhaps Confucius had too much faith in his fellow humans, and Plato too little. Perhaps they were both right, and both wrong. One thing is certain: for good or ill, we cannot understand Chinese thought and behavior without understanding Confucius, and Western philosophy makes little sense unless we start by discussing the ideas of Plato. And to be a truly educated citizen in the twenty-first century, we need to know both of these thinkers.

Notes

1. Karl Jaspers, *The Great Philosophers,* vol. I (New York: Harcourt, Brace and World, 1962), 51.
2. "Introduction" to *Analects,* translated with notes by Simon Leys (New York: Norton, 1997), xvi.
3. Since there are many translations of both the *Analects* and Plato's *Republic,* passages in these works are generally divided by numbers, like chapters and verses in the *Bible.* See *Analects,* 5.12 (chapter 5, passage 12): "I would not want to do to others what I do not want them to do me"; this is also repeated in 12.2, and 15.24. All passages from the *Analects* are taken from the translation by Simon Leys referred to above.
4. *Analects,* 6.27.
5. *Analects,* 12.16 and 14.41; see also 12.19–20.
6. See *Sources of Chinese Tradition,* vol. I, compiled by Wm. Theodore De Bary, Wing-Tsit Chan, and Burton Watson (New York: Columbia University Press, 1960), 120.
7. For the full text of this passage, see *The Ways of Religion: An Introduction to the Major Traditions,* 2d ed., edited by Roger Eastman (New York: Oxford University Press, 1993), 175.
8. C. Muller, translator, *Mencius,* n.d. <http://www2.gol.com/user. . . muller/contao/mencius.htm> (November 15, 1996). Many other translations are available.
9. See *Analects,* 13.15: In responding to the question: "Is there one single maxim that could ruin a country? [Confucius said] 'The only pleasure of being a prince is never having to suffer contradiction. If you are right and no one contradicts you, that's fine; but if you are wrong and no one contradicts you—is this not almost a case of 'one single maxim that could ruin a country'?"
10. See chapter 5 of this book on Thucydides and Sima Qian for a brief description of this conflict.
11. William S. Sahakian and Mabel Lewis Sahakian, *Plato* (New York: Twayne, 1977), 31–37.
12. See *Republic,* passages 435–442. All references to *Republic* are from the translation by Robin Waterfield (New York: Barnes and Noble, 1996). See also Sahakian, *Plato,* 80.
13. Plato, *Republic,* 514a–518b.
14. Ibid., 476d, 474b–c.
15. Ibid., 535a–b, 456–460. See chapter 7, "Women, Children, and Warfare" in Waterfield's *Republic* for Plato's description of relations between the sexes in the guardian class.
16. Ibid., 382c–d, 389b–c, 414d–e, 525–534. Also Sahakian, *Plato,* 114–121.
17. Ibid., 415a.

18. See R. Brambrough, ed., *Plato, Popper, and Politics* (Cambridge: W. Heffer & Sons, 1967) and T. L. Thorson, ed., *Plato: Totalitarian or Democrat?* (Englewood Cliffs, NJ: Prentice-Hall, 1963). While Plato's views on such things as communal property and sex were shocking to many—in his day as well as ours—it is anachronistic (out of place chronologically) to blame him for the excesses of twentieth-century Hitlers and Stalins. If nothing else, the fundamental goal of Plato—how to promote the good life—contrasted with the fundamental goal of the modern totalitarian dictators, which was power.

19. See "Laws," trans. A. E. Taylor, in *The Collected Dialogues of Plato,* ed. Edith Hamilton and Huntingdon Cairns (Princeton: Princeton University Press, 1961), 1225–1513.

Further Reading

The Analects of Confucius. Translation and notes by SIMON LEYS. New York: Norton, 1997. A lively translation with a useful introduction and very interesting endnotes.

DAWSON, RAYMOND. *Confucius.* New York: Hill and Wang, 1981. A short, readable introduction to the life and ideas of Confucius.

SAHAKIAN, WILLIAM S., and MABLE LEWIS SAHAKIAN. *Plato.* New York: Twayne, 1977. A good place to start reading about Plato's life and ideas. Brief and clear.

PLATO. *Republic.* Translated by Robin Waterfield. New York: Barnes and Noble, 1996. Perhaps the most readable translation of this work; there are many others available. Also has a useful introduction.

CHAPTER 4

Mahavira and Diogenes: Unconventional Men

Can a man challenge the behavior and values of the people in his society and still remain a part of that society? (Or when is a misfit not really a misfit?) Why did self-reliance and individualism take different forms in these Eastern and Western societies? What characteristics did these men share?

We have all known people who did not seem to fit into the world in which they lived, who said "inappropriate" things, acted "funny," and generally challenged our ideas of what was socially proper. While we often write off such people as "misfits," we also often admire the social rebels—for such people can say or do things we are unable or afraid to say or do. They can provoke us to challenge our own beliefs and standards, and they can lead us deeper within ourselves.

Two such unconventional individuals, whose lives posed a creative challenge to their respective societies, were Mahavira (ca. 540–468 B.C.E.), the founder of the Jain religion in India, and Diogenes of Sinope (ca. 412–323 B.C.E.), an early Cynic philosopher who lived in the Greek world of Plato and Alexander the Great. Both men challenged their society—by scorning dominant behaviors. Both withdrew into a life of simplicity and physical hardship, but neither was able to detach himself completely from the society whose materialism and stupidities he rejected. Mahavira wandered homeless throughout India as a begging monk for thirty years, trying to free his soul from all attachments to the world. Yet he managed to establish an order of monks that grew into a full-fledged religion which has survived to our day. Diogenes was also homeless, an inhabitant of the cities of Athens and Corinth who used an old pottery jar or water cask for shelter in bad weather. Yet he did not leave either city or its people, preferring to remain a "thorn in their side," shouting insults to passers-by and puncturing the pretensions of the wealthy and powerful with witty remarks that are the stuff of legend. Both individualists left the mainstream of life but kept their small boats moored close enough to the channel to make travelers uncomfortably aware they were being watched.

Like other ancient leaders who became spiritual achievers, Mahavira (a title meaning "great hero"; his given name was Vardhamma) was the son of noble parents. His father was a minor ruler in the region of Mogadsh in northern India when Mahavira was born. Although Jain traditions place his birth in the year 599, many scholars believe the year 540 is more accurate. There is no doubt, however, that this sensitive young man was a product of the intellectually creative fifth and sixth centuries, the period of Buddha and Confucius in the East and of Plato in the West. Little is known of Mahavira's childhood, except that he had an older brother. One legend tells of how the young Vardhamma subdued a terrifying snake by his "courage and peaceful aura." Beyond this, "we know virtually nothing."[1]

Mahavira's spiritual development followed a pattern similar to that of other major religious leaders such as Zoroaster and Buddha. At age thirty, he left his wife and child in order to seek truth by following the life of a wandering hermit. After following this life for twelve years, Mahavira had a spiritual awakening and became a *kevalin* (perfected soul) or a *jina* (conqueror—from which the name of the religion, Jainism, is taken). For the next thirty years, he traveled about India, organizing his disciples into an order of monks, preaching to them and to his "lay" followers, practicing severe asceticism, and following the principle of *ahimsa*—non-violence to all living things. It was taking these two practices of asceticism and *ahimsa* to the extreme that made Mahavira an unconventional man. While traditional Hinduism had long admired the holy man who retreated to the forest, fasted, and meditated on the nature of ultimate truth as a way to attain salvation, no one before or since Mahavira pushed the principle of self-denial as far as he and his disciples did. Mahavira renounced the things we would expect a holy man to renounce (killing, lying, greed, sexual pleasure, and property) and much more. An early Jain scripture reports that, when Mahavira's robe fell into shreds after a year of walking, he simply went naked—at least during the dry season. He also refused to use cold water, clean his teeth, brush vermin from his body, or scratch himself (for fear of killing living things). When people, alarmed by his appearance and behavior, abused him verbally and beat him with sticks, he refused medical treatment, "humbled himself and bore pain, free from desire." When Mahavira did take shelter, he seldom stayed in the same place more than one night, and he spent many nights sleeping in cemeteries, gardens, or abandoned buildings.[2]

All this physical self-punishment seems neurotic to us and was even rejected by Mahavira's contemporary, the Buddha, who preached a "middle way" between a life of pleasure and one of severe self-denial, yet it made sense to this man who believed that *any* attachment whatsoever to worldly things would hinder one's salvation. For Mahavira, this asceticism, or self-denial, was intimately related to the equally severe practice of *ahimsa*, which forbade *any* violence to *any* living thing. *Ahimsa* led Mahavira to sweep the ground before him with a small broom so that he would not accidentally step on any small creatures. He also instructed his early followers to place a cloth in front of their faces when they spoke in order to prevent "tiny forms of life" from accidentally entering the nose and mouth and being injured. Jain monks would also not eat at night, since preparing food by lamp light would attract insects that would be harmed.[3]

Practicing *ahimsa* also helped the Jain monk avoid evil by avoiding attachment to material things. Like other Indians, Mahavira believed that evil deeds resulted in evil spiritual consequences (bad karma), which could keep one's soul imprisoned in the material body for many lifetimes. Mahavira interpreted this dogma, as he did the principle of *ahimsa*, very literally. He told his followers that the evil they did and the attachments they pursued would turn into bad karma, which would literally "cling to the soul" and weigh it down so that it could not float free of their body when they died. One could burn off this spiritual cholesterol in somewhat the same way we get rid of its physical counterpart [fatty substances in the blood]—by fasting. It was reported that Mahavira would go months without drinking and ate very sparingly: "Sometimes he ate only the sixth meal, or the eighth, the tenth, the twelfth; without desires, persevering in meditation."[4] Mahavira pursued his principles to their logical conclusion, dying at age seventy-two by starving himself to death.

Perhaps the most interesting thing about the teachings of Mahavira is their emphasis on self-reliance. He rejected the idea that a noble birth, a high place in society, or even the favor of a god could help a person find happiness or salvation. Even prayer was pointless, and Mahavira dismissed the scriptures and rituals of Hinduism as unnecessary. Only the individual could save him- or herself, and only by practicing extreme asceticism. Yet, despite this emphasis on the individual, Mahavira and his followers (one source reports that he had half a million by his death) did not hesitate to prescribe numerous and exacting rules for those who wished to follow the path of the Great Hero. A Jain monk started his career with a food bowl, two small water pots, a broom, a napkin, and a loin-cloth. Except during the rainy season, he was not allowed to stay more than three nights in one village, and, even then, following the example of Mahavira, the building where he slept could not be an inhabited one. Jain monks divided the day into four periods, and they were given four duties: meditation, individual study, teaching of Jain beliefs to others, and food collection. Each of these activities was hedged with further rules and regulations. A monk could eat only thirty-two mouthfuls of food a day, for example, and each mouthful could only be the size of a small bird's egg.[5] Although all of these rules existed to promote spiritual freedom, they did this in a society in which social ties had always been important. The punishment of the body, or external asceticism, was paralleled by an "internal asceticism," an emphasis on the virtues of submission, decorum, willingness to serve, and surrender to authority.[6] By practicing these virtues, one could free oneself from the world of matter, while at the same time reassuring one's neighbors that such eccentricities would not disrupt their society.

Mahavira wished to become self-reliant and independent of the world, without seeking to change it; after all, one could only change oneself. This was a very Indian idea, even though Mahavira pushed it further than did his Hindu or Buddhist contemporaries. Self-knowledge and self-reliance were just as important to the Greek Cynic philosopher Diogenes as they had been to Mahavira. There is even an outside chance that Diogenes may have heard of the naked Indian ascetic. In ancient times, the city of Sinope on the Black Sea, where Diogenes was born, was the terminus of a trade route that brought goods from India through the Persian Gulf to Europe. Many of the beliefs and practices developed by Diogenes or attributed to him, things such as indifference to wealth, endurance of material hardship, and the importance of simplicity, were similar to those of Mahavira. Because of this, one scholar has inferred that some Indian ideas were carried along the trade route from northern India to the Mediterranean world.[7] While it is certainly true that the behavior of Diogenes was as unconventional as that of Mahavira, the exact nature of the challenge he posed to his contemporaries was different—as fifth-century Greece was different from fifth-century India.

In the first place, Diogenes of Sinope was more clearly in rebellion against the behavior of his day than was Mahavira, who was, after all, merely taking standard Indian convictions to their logical conclusions. Almost all the stories told about Diogenes suggest that he was a wise but angry man. The word *Cynic,* which became the name of the philosophical school that Diogenes helped establish, came from the Greek word for dog. Diogenes was called "the dog" because of his biting wit and snappish behavior. We call a person cynical today if he or she is distrustful of human motives and has a generally low opinion of humankind. The modern word *cynic* exactly describes the behavior of Diogenes, who once tried to beg alms from a statue and, when questioned by a passer-by on his strange behavior, said that he was doing this in order to get practice in being refused.[8]

Perhaps we would be angry, too, if we were unfairly exiled from our hometown, as Diogenes may have been. Hikesias, father of Diogenes, was a prominent citizen and, for a time, the treasurer or banker of the prosperous Greek trading city of Sinope. While in this position, he systematically defaced some counterfeit coins by making gashes in them with a chisel. Although he did this in order to stabilize the city's currency, he was later accused—perhaps by political enemies—of "tampering with the coinage" and put in jail. His son and assistant, Diogenes, was exiled from Sinope; he went to Athens "embittered, the victim of spite and injustice . . . hating everything and everyone," in the words of one scholar.[9] While this assessment of the personality of Diogenes may be too harsh, there is no doubt that this man lived a life of self-sufficiency and poverty, not in order to attain holiness or salvation but in order to acquire virtue and be a standing reproach to his fellow citizens. If Diogenes was mad, there was a method to his madness. He wanted to make his fellow Athenians and Corinthians think. He insulted them only to get their attention.

But insult them he did! Seeing the child of a prostitute throwing rocks into a crowd, he warned him to be careful or he'd hit his father. When he saw a bad archer practicing one day, he sat down near the target "in order not to get hit." On another occasion, he asked a man who was discussing heavenly bodies with great authority: "How many days were you in coming from the sky?" This last barb shows how much Diogenes enjoyed deflating the ego of anyone—from peasant to king—who displayed self-importance. One day a bad-tempered man from whom Diogenes was begging alms offered to give the philosopher some money "if you can persuade me." "If I could have persuaded you," said Diogenes, "I would have persuaded you to hang yourself." But Diogenes was not interested in merely insulting people. He really wanted his "victims" (and other listeners) to examine their lives. In the tradition of the famous questioner Socrates, his contemporary, he used the pungent phrase and the pointed question in order to teach. A famous story about the meeting between Diogenes and world conqueror Alexander the Great in 336 makes this point. When Diogenes did not greet the great king at the city gates of Corinth, Alexander sought out Diogenes (by now a tourist attraction in his pottery jar) and told him he could give him anything he wanted. Diogenes asked him to please stand aside, since he was blocking the sunlight. It is said that Alexander remarked as he left, "If I were not Alexander, I would choose to be Diogenes."[10] Another version of their meeting contains the following exchange:

DIOGENES: "What, your majesty, is your greatest desire at present?"
ALEXANDER: "To subjugate Greece."
DIOGENES: "And after you have subjugated Greece?"
ALEXANDER: "I will subjugate Asia Minor."
DIOGENES: "And after that?"
ALEXANDER: "I will subjugate the world."
DIOGENES: "And after that?"
ALEXANDER: "I plan to relax and enjoy myself."
DIOGENES: "Why not save yourself all the trouble by relaxing and
    enjoying yourself right now?"[11]

The encounter, real or imagined, between Diogenes and Alexander emphasizes the importance of simplicity and self-examination to Diogenes. Pursuing self-mastery, Diogenes punished his body in ways that Mahavira might have found congenial. In addition to going nearly naked and living on the streets of Corinth in a cracked pottery jar, Diogenes practiced self-control by embracing statues in the winter and rolling his vat along the hot sand in the summer. Yet, if Diogenes was an ascetic, his brand of physical self-denial was different from that of Mahavira. The Indian holy man tried to detach himself from the material world for a specific, immediate reason: attachment to things created bad karma, which kept the soul from achieving salvation. For Diogenes, bodily comforts were not necessarily evil in themselves, but they were symbols of reliance on others. Depending upon others for happiness was the real evil for this Greek thinker. The truly wise person required nothing that nature did not already provide. This is why Diogenes even threw away his drinking cup when he saw a young boy outdo him "in plainness of living" by drinking water from his cupped hands.[12] This is also why Diogenes made fun of the wealthy, the intellectually important (e.g., Plato), and the politically powerful. People in each of these categories were in danger of losing their personal, interior freedom, something that would happen if they were to rely on the good will, money, or praise of others.

This self-reliance made Diogenes one of the Western world's first great individualists. But his individualism was also different from that of the great Indian teachers, Mahavira and Buddha. They chose to withdraw; he chose to confront. They chose personal "religious" salvation; he chose personal ethical autonomy. The present was more important than the afterlife to the Greeks. Diogenes' ideal of independence had little to do with karma; it was more secular but also stopped short of our modern ideals of personal political rights or independence. This last point is illustrated by the story of how Diogenes got from Athens to Corinth. After residing in Athens for a number of years, the philosopher was captured by pirates while on a voyage to Aegina and was taken to Crete to be sold as a slave. When asked what he was proficient in, he answered:

> "In ruling men." He then looked over the crowd gathered for the slave auction, spotted a wealthy-looking fellow, and said: "Sell me to this man; he needs a master."[13]

The wealthy Corinthian, a man named Xeniades, bought Diogenes and took him home, where the philosopher spent the last years of his life tutoring the sons of his master. Diogenes did not mind being a slave because external freedom, like today's highly regarded "financial independence," meant little to him. The most important freedom to Diogenes was the freedom to make his own moral decisions. His poverty and unconventional lifestyle helped him preserve this freedom.

Emphasis on freedom does not itself explain the general surliness and sarcasm of this famous Cynic. Diogenes once said that the most beautiful thing in the world was freedom of speech; he used this freedom to insult and provoke. A modern clinical psychologist would probably tell us that this man's insults were, at least in part, displaced resentment at his treatment by the citizens of Sinope. Diogenes also may have enjoyed the attention that his sharp tongue and eccentric life brought him. While these things may be true, it is also likely that the barbs and witticisms for which he was famous were an integral part of his message. When he said that gold was pale, for example, because so many people were plotting against it, or when he called an ignorant rich man "the sheep with the golden fleece," this got people's attention and gave them something worth remembering and repeating—an important consideration in an age when most people were illiterate. His jeers and jokes had another purpose as well. In suggesting that the study of music, geometry, and astronomy was unnecessary, in advocating sharing of wives ("recognizing no other marriage than the union of the man who persuades with the woman who consents"), and in saying that the wine he enjoyed most was someone else's, Diogenes was not merely trying to shock people.[14] He was telling his contemporaries that everything—intellectual skills, property, even other people—could be taken lightly because they were less than ultimate, especially to the person who sought moral independence.

It is clear that Diogenes found it important both to live in a particular way and to make sure that his fellow citizens knew why he was living the way he was. He felt called to awaken others to the noble life of simple self-sufficiency that he had come to appreciate. Mahavira had earlier felt that same urge to share his good news with others. Thus, he founded his order of monks and his religion. This missionary impulse on the part of both of these famous individualists is the first reason we have to think twice before calling them misfits. We might also note that true misfits would not have been remembered. It is only because the lives and words of these men challenged the people of their day that they became part of the historical record. A genuine neurotic would not reflect social values as clearly as these men did.

Mahavira and Diogenes were lucky that each lived in a society that accepted unusual behavior. The wandering *sadhu*, or holy man, had been a part of Hindu tradition for centuries before Mahavira began his career. The pointed comments of Diogenes probably did not bother Athenians excessively because this was the city, after all, where Western people first began to ask critical questions about nature, both human and physical. Both Mahavira and Diogenes were unconventional men but both were products of their cultures. The self-reliance preached by Mahavira was a distinctly Indian product, nurtured by the holy books and Hindu practices of that subcontinent. He fertilized a spiritual plant that already existed. The less gentle type of self-reliance preached by Diogenes was as much Greek as *ahimsa* was Indian. In his own brash way, Diogenes the Cynic confirmed and advanced the skeptical, questioning spirit of classical Greece. However strange his life, his notions of moral self-sufficiency could not ultimately disturb a society in which humans (not the gods) were "the measure of all things."

To be unconventional is necessarily to be part of your time and place whose values you choose to ignore. It can be unconventional to take the truth quite literally, as both Mahavira and Diogenes did. If a rich person is owned by his or her possessions, then he or she should get rid of them. If living according to nature is a good thing, then do it—even if it means going naked or living in an old pottery jar. If humanity is ennobled by suffering, then one should punish the body, not just a little for show, but as much as possible. These were some of the things that this Hindu ascetic and Greek gadfly said that made them unconventional—but memorable.

One story about the death of Diogenes tells us that the eighty-nine-year-old philosopher died in a Corinth gymnasium by voluntarily holding his breath. He had supposedly left instructions that his body be thrown into a ditch and covered with a little dirt.[15] Diogenes may not have died this way, just as Mahavira may not have died by voluntarily starving himself to death. The fact that these stories, whether true or not, are told and believed, is itself a tribute to the sincerity and similarity of these two men who thought and acted "otherwise."

Notes

1. Padmanabh S. Jaina, *The Jaina Path of Purification* (Berkeley: University of California Press, 1979), 6–11.

2. Akaranga-sutra, part I, in *Sacred Books of the East* (Oxford: Oxford University Press, 1884), 85–87; see also Bimala Churn Law, *Mahavira: His Life and Teaching* (London: Luzac and Co., 1937), 21–23.

3. Walter Schubring, *The Religion of the Jainas*, trans. Anmulyachandra Sen and T. C. Burke (Calcutta: Sanskrit College, 1966), 27; Amrit Chandra Acharya, *Sacred Books of the Jains*, vol. IV, *Purusartha Siddhupaya* (Lucknow, India: Central Jaina Publishing House, 1933), 43–44.

4. Jaina, *Jaina Path of Purification*, 113; Akaranga-sutra, part I, in *Sacred Books of the East*, 87.

5. Denise Carmody and John Carmody, *Eastern Ways to the Center: An Introduction to the Religions of Asia*, 2d ed. (Belmont, CA: Wadsworth Publishing Co., 1992), 25–26; Schubring, *Religion of the Jainas*, 27–28; Louis Renou, *Religions of Ancient India* (New York: Schocken Books, 1968), 126–127.

6. Schubring, *Religion of the Jainas*, 30–31.

7. Ferrand Sayre, *Diogenes of Sinope: A Study of Greek Cynicism* (Baltimore: J. H. Furst, 1938), 39–45.

8. Ibid., 7. This story, like many others about Diogenes, comes from the accounts of Diogenes Laertius (no relation), a third-century (A.D.) compiler of information about famous philosophers. See Diogenes Laertius, "Diogenes," in *Lives of Eminent Philosophers*, II, trans. R. D. Hicks (Cambridge, MA: Harvard University Press, 1925), 23–84. It is impossible to verify many of the anecdotes and tales told of Diogenes; some are legends or parables created later to illustrate the teachings of later Cynic philosophers. The stories do present a consistent view of Diogenes, however, and they show that later thinkers found value in his unconventional life and thought.

9. Charles Seltman, "Diogenes: The Original Cynic," *History Today*, vol. VI, No. 2 (February 1956), 110–115.

10. Diogenes Laertius, *Lives of Eminent Philosophers*, 41, 61, 63, 69; Plutarch, *Eight Great Lives*, ed. C. A. Robinson, Jr. (New York: Holt, Rinehart and Winston, 1960), 76.

11. "Diogenes," in *Biographical Encyclopedia of Philosophy* (Garden City, NY: Doubleday and Company, 1965), 76.

12. Diogenes Laertius, *Lives of Eminent Philosophers*, 39.

13. Ibid., 77.

14. Ibid., 49, 53, 57, 73, 75.

15. Ibid., 79–81.

Further Reading

LAERTIUS, DIOGENES. *Lives of Eminent Philosophers,* vol. II. Trans. R. D. Hicks. Cambridge, MA: Harvard University Press, 1925, 23–84. Best source for anecdotes about Diogenes.

LAW, BIMALA CHURN. *Mahavira: His Life and Teaching.* London: Luzac and Co., 1937. One of the few readable accounts of Mahavira in English. Also see essays in encyclopedias and textbooks on world religions.

SELTMAN, CHARLES. "Diogenes: The Original Cynic" *History Today* (February 1956): 110–115. Very readable.

CHAPTER 5

Thucydides and Sima Qian: Learning from the Past

Why do we keep records of the past? How do historical works reflect the values of writers and their cultures? Is one kind of history better than another?

These two ancient historians had a sense of drama. In *Records of the Grand Historian* by Sima Qian (145–86? B.C.E.), we find the loyal servants and scheming traitors, the jealous women and exuberant men of China during the Qin and early Han dynasties. One of these was the first Han emperor, Liu Bang, who had spent years as a rebel general, clawing his way to the top. At a banquet to celebrate the completion of his new palace, he offered a toast to his father: "You, my father, always used to consider me a worthless fellow who could never look after the family fortune and had not half the industry of my older brother Zhong. Now that my labors are completed, which of us has accomplished more, Zhong or I?" How would you expect the audience to react? "All the officials in the hall shouted 'Long life!' and roared with merriment," according to Sima Qian.[1]

Thucydides (459?–402? B.C.E.) wrote his *History of the Peloponnesian War* as a dramatic tale of the war for ultimate power in Greece between the powerful city-state (polis) of Athens and its arch-rival, Sparta. This conflict was inspired, Thucydides tells us, by "the growth of the power of Athens and the alarm which this inspired in Sparta." We see Athens slowly destroyed, as much by its own mistakes and arrogance as by its enemies. As both a historian and the Western world's first political scientist, Thucydides is famous for examining how political power was used during what he saw as the greatest war in Greek history, and how it might be used in the future.[2]

Their sense of what made for good reading is not the only quality these historians shared. Both wanted to preserve the deeds of great men, which they did by creating speeches that they put in the mouths of their characters. Neither man had much interest in supernatural explanations of events, but both frequently made moral judgments. Both Sima Qian and Thucydides believed that historical events were not arbitrary but followed a pattern. While Thucydides was more interested in broader social forces than was Sima Qian, neither ignored the colorful individuals who make the past exciting.

Finally, each man suffered misfortune, though Sima Qian's was greater. Thucydides was an Athenian general during the early years of the Peloponnesian War; he was exiled for twenty years after losing a battle. Sima Qian, while serving as "Grand Historian" during the reign of Han Emperor Wu (114–87 B.C.E.), fell into disfavor with the ruler when he unwisely defended a general who had been defeated by the Xiongnu (Huns). Sentenced to die for disloyalty, his poor family was unable to pay the large fine necessary for a pardon in such cases. So Sima Qian—perhaps at his own suggestion—was castrated as an alternative to execution.[3]

Both Thucydides and Sima Qian were active in the ruling class of their respective states. Beyond this, we know very little about their lives. Thucydides came from an aristocratic family that owned gold mines in Thrace on the northern coast of the Aegean Sea. He used income from these holdings to support himself after he went to Athens. Thucydides became a general in 424 B.C.E., and that same year was defeated and exiled. He wrote most of his history during the remainder of the war and returned to Athens in 404 B.C.E., dying several years later, with the work unfinished.[4] Sima Qian tells us in a short biography included as the final chapter of his work that he was born at Longmen in the north and as a youth "plowed and pastured on the sunny side of the hills along the river." At the age of ten, he said, "he could read the old writings." Sima Qian, a strong Confucianist, said in his biography that his father, a court historian, made him promise to continue his work. Sima Qian also complained bitterly about his own castration in a letter to a friend, Ren An. Calling himself a "remnant of saw and blade," Sima Qian strongly denied the charges made against him. He justified his decision to accept castration over death because death would have prevented him from completing his history, which he hoped would "be handed down to men who will appreciate it. . . ."[5]

The differences between these two men are as significant as their similarities. Both wanted to leave an honest record of the past, but Thucydides, in the spirit of rational inquiry characteristic of the Greeks, wanted to understand *why* people behave as they do, while Sima Qian wanted to explain *how* people *ought* to behave. This tells us something about the different outlook of Greek and Chinese societies. Like his predecessor, Herodotus, who wrote a massive history of the early fifth-century wars between Greece and Persia, Thucydides investigated the past to discover truth and to better analyze human nature. Sima Qian, the "father" of Chinese history, as Herodotus and Thucydides were of Western history, was less interested in discovering truth than in promoting moral actions and preserving traditions. In China, where honoring one's family was important, it was necessary to preserve knowledge of the past so that "one's good deeds would be handed down to later generations and thus bring credit to one's ancestors."[6] Sima Qian was convinced that Confucius had adequately understood human nature; therefore, he already knew why people behaved as they did. The important thing was to record as many examples of good and bad behavior as he could, so that people in the future would know what to imitate and what to avoid.[7]

Because of these different outlooks, the emphasis in Chinese history was on *what happened,* while the Greek writers wanted to know both what happened and *why it happened.* Both peoples wanted to learn from the past, but they wanted to learn slightly different things. Thucydides told the story of his "great war" in hopes that people might learn to avoid causes of war in the future. Sima Qian concentrated on the lives of individuals in order to promote ethical behavior in the future. As a good Confucian, he assumed that the state would be healthy if people behaved properly. While not ignoring individuals, Thucydides also explored how humans acting collectively in political bodies reacted under pressure.

Because of their different aims, the two historians organized their histories differently. Because Thucydides wrote a single, long narrative, something we find familiar, it is best to look at his work first. To set the stage, we need to know that, when the Persians tried to conquer Greece in the early fifth century, Athens and Sparta led the other Greek cities in defeating them. During these wars, Athens, located on the Attic peninsula in eastern Greece, built up a large navy, and, after the Persians were defeated in 479 B.C.E., many Greek cities joined Athens in the Delian League. Athens quickly used its naval power to turn the league into an Athenian empire, insisting that the members pay tribute to Athens and punishing cities that tried to withdraw. Sparta, located in southern Greece (the Peloponnesus), built up its alliance system in response to the growing power of Athens.

It was the conflict between these two powerful city-states between 431 and 404 B.C.E. that is the subject of *History of the Peloponnesian War*. This war, as Thucydides understood it, was not just a struggle over control of Greece. It was a battle between competing political systems. Athens was a democratic state, with thirty thousand voting male citizens (10 percent of the population) organized into geographic districts known as *demes*, from which we get our word *democracy*. Sparta was a military state governed by aristocratic families who dominated a subject population of *helots*, conquered peoples who produced food and other necessities for the citizens. This allowed (some would say forced) Spartan males between the ages of seven and thirty to live in barracks.[8] Athens had the best navy in Greece, and Sparta an excellent infantry force and many allies. This great conflict of both ideas and men began in 431 B.C.E., when the Thebans, allies of Sparta, attacked the city of Plataea, an ally of Athens.

Thucydides' account shows the military complexity of the conflict, which need only be summarized here. During the first ten years of the war, until a truce in 421 B.C.E., the Spartans and their allies invaded Attica five times. The fighting forced many of the residents of Attica (some three hundred thousand people) inside the city walls of Athens. This may have contributed to the plague in Athens in 429 B.C.E. Thucydides, who contracted it and survived, described its symptoms carefully so that it "may be recognized . . . if it should ever break out again."[9] Despite these setbacks, the Athenians fought back, holding their empire together in the face of repeated Spartan attacks. A turning point of sorts occurred in 415–414 B.C.E., when the Athenians, still facing enemies at home, sent a huge force to Sicily, over one thousand miles from Athens, in a foolish attempt to conquer the dominant city-state of Syracuse and add the island to its empire. The expedition was a disaster, as Syracusans joined Spartan troops, rushed to the island, and defeated the Athenians. Although fighting continued for ten more years, Athens was doomed. In the final years, the Spartans accepted help from Persian Governor Tissaphernes, and the democratic government at Athens was temporarily overthrown by an aristocratic one. Though Thucydides' *History* ends in 411 B.C.E., the Athenians were not finally defeated until their fleet was captured in 405 B.C.E.; the city itself was blockaded and surrendered in 404 B.C.E.

Thucydides' account of the military victories and defeats of these years are not the most interesting feature of his history. More important are the many speeches which he used to analyze the decisions made by Athens. Several were delivered by Pericles, the Athenian leader early in the war. On the eve of war, he urged the Athenians to fight, lest the Spartans think them weak, setting a tone that would last throughout the war. Thucydides also inserted in his narrative the famous Funeral Oration, in which Pericles commemorated those who had fallen in the first year of the war. Pericles praised the laws and the freedom of Athenian citizens to "live exactly as we please," unlike the Spartans who must exclude foreigners and live "by a painful [military] discipline." Indeed, he announced, Athens set the pattern for democratic government and was "the school of Hellas" [Greece]; Athens ruled others only by merit and by the courage of its soldiers, who regarded cowardice as worse than death.[10] However, after the plague and a second Spartan invasion of Attica, the Athenians "began to find fault with Pericles . . . and became eager to come to terms with Sparta." Pericles urged them to take heart and warned them that they could not sue for peace without losing their empire. In a statement of remarkable honesty and insight, he told his fellow citizens that their empire was "to speak somewhat plainly, a tyranny; to take it perhaps was wrong, but to let it go is unsafe." Although Pericles did convince the Athenians not to sue for peace at that time, he was unable to convince them to win by "wait[ing] quietly . . . pay[ing] attention to their marine [forces]" and "attempt[ing] no new conquests." Instead, they "allowed private ambitions . . . to lead them into projects unjust both to themselves and to their allies [which] entailed certain disaster."[11]

The most important of these unjust projects was the expedition to Sicily in 415 B.C.E., a blunder caused by the willingness of an Athenian leader, Alcibiades, to cater to the "whims of the multitude" and promise them an easy victory. Alcibiades, ambitious and greedy, according to Thucydides, convinced the Athenians that the conquest of Sicily would humble the Spartans by showing them that the men of Athens were brave enough to embark on a conquest far from home, even while still threatened by the cities of the Peloponnese. Nicias, an Athenian opponent of the arrogant and loose-living Alcibiades, feared this greed for conquest and tried without success to warn his fellow citizens against the Sicilian expedition, arguing that this campaign would give Sparta another chance to attack them.[12] Alcibiades prevailed, however, and, when the expedition ended in Athenian defeat two years later, Nicias, "a man who, of all the Hellenes in my time, least deserved such a fate," was "butchered" by the Syracusans after he surrendered.[13] After the defeat of the Athenian forces in Sicily, Alcibiades became a traitor, joining with the Spartans and Persians to encourage the revolt of the cities and island under Athenian control in Asia Minor. When the Athenians decided that they needed Persian help to defeat Sparta, they forgave Alcibiades his treason and recalled him in hopes of winning Persian help. He led the city to some victories between 410 B.C.E. and 406 B.C.E. but finally fell into disgrace just two years before the final Athenian capitulation to Sparta.[14]

Thucydides had mixed feelings about democracy, since it allowed opportunists such as Alcibiades to manipulate the majority with clever words and could result in the death of men of wisdom and integrity such as Nicias. Yet he also recognized that democracy gave people a stake in their government and promoted unity and patriotism. However, for Thucydides, the deeper questions were not so much about the forms of government as they were about political power itself. Did the misuse of power corrupt the Athenians and lead to their downfall? Was Thucydides distrustful of political power in democratic settings only, or was he pessimistic about the ability of all people to use power wisely? Thucydides' final judgments about power are mixed, causing much debate by scholars.[15] At times, he seemed to say that power always tended to corrupt people. At other times, he seemed to believe that power was itself neutral and could be used for good or evil purposes. Yet it seems clear that Thucydides believed that war was caused by fear, that fear led to poor decisions, especially in a democracy, and often to civil war (*stasis*). All this caused great suffering and could lead to defeat.

Some parts of Thucydides' *History of the Peloponnesian War* were written at the end of his life and inserted in the original narrative.[16] These additions contain the more reflective comments by this historian/participant. The speech of Pericles which warned against "unjust projects" was one such addition. Other passages added to the text later also make judgments about power. In 427 B.C.E., for example, the city-state of Corcyra, divided between a democratic pro-Athenian faction and an oligarchic pro-Spartan faction, was "saved" by an Athenian fleet. Immediately, a civil war broke out in which the Athenian faction slew its enemies. Thucydides' comment on how "human nature" led to such bloodshed was pointed. "War is a stern teacher; in depriving them of the power of easily satisfying their daily wants, it brings most people's minds down to the level of their actual circumstances."[17] War also brought envy and revenge to the surface, he added, and "frantic violence became the attribute of manliness; cautious plotting a justifiable means of self-defense." Those who engaged in treachery were considered clever, and soon all trust disappeared. Perhaps this disillusionment about war caused by the final Athenian defeat was what motivated Thucydides to refer to "the general law of decay" in the last speech delivered by Pericles.[18]

Thucydides used his *History* to make moral points. Sima Qian also wrote to leave moral lessons, but his were told largely through the lives of individuals. Consider this tale about Liu Bang, the Han emperor, and his father, whom we met in the opening paragraph of this essay. Even after becoming emperor, Liu Bang visited his father weekly, deferring to him as called for by proper Confucian etiquette. After one of these visits, the father's steward reminded the older man that his son was now emperor, and that it did not look right for "the ruler of men" to be humbling himself before "one of his subjects." Taking the hint, when Bang visited next, his father met him with broom in hand "as a sign of servitude." The emperor was so pleased that he gave his father the title "Grand Supreme Emperor" and slipped the steward 500 gold coins.[19] Aside from the obvious emphasis on Confucian values and on the respect due the ruler, this story also reveals the subtlety that has marked Chinese culture for several millennia.

The first thing we notice about *Records of the Grand Historian*, however, is not the stories or moral tales but the unusual way in which the work is organized. Instead of recounting the history of ancient China to the Han dynasty of his day in chronological order, Sima Qian divided his 130 chapters as follows:

- "basic annals" (*ben ji*)—a year-by-year chronicle of succession of rulers and political events
- "chronological tables" (*nian biao*)—synchronizing the dates of the states of the Zhou dynasty and listing the dates when divisions of the Han state were established, changed, or abolished
- "treatises" (*shu*)—essays on topics important to rulers such as court ceremonies, the calendar, "water control, and state control over the economy"
- "hereditary houses" (*shi ja*)—chronological accounts of late Zhou rulers, early Han kings, Chen She, an early rebel against the Qin, and Confucius
- "memoirs" (*lie zhuan*)—biographies of individuals or groups of individuals[20]

Records contains no index, and many individuals are mentioned in more than one chapter. The only way to "get all the facts" about a particular event or person is to read the entire work, some 526,000 characters, four times as long as Thucydides' *History*. While this organization has clear disadvantages for those of us used to a clear story line, it has some advantages as well. All the chapters are short, so the work is arranged somewhat like a filing system for a busy bureaucrat. Does the emperor want to check out the meaning of a shooting star? He can check the treatise on astronomy and quickly find some information. If the ruler is having a problem with one of the officials from the state of Wu, he can pull the treatise on that state and quickly review relations between that kingdom and the Han rulers in recent centuries.[21]

Another advantage of his organization is that it allowed readers to look at the same event or person from many perspectives. For example, Wei Bao, a member of the royal family of the state of Wei, joined Liu Bang in 206 B.C.E. in his revolt against the collapsing Qin dynasty but deserted him a year later. Wei Bao's "defection" is discussed in nine chapters of the *Records*, and each time his motives are explained slightly differently. "The Basic Annals of Gaozu" [official title of the first Han ruler] simply mentioned that Wei Bao went home to take care of his aging parents, revolted against the Han forces, and allied himself with the state of Chu, Han's rival. The chapter titled "The Biographies of Wei Bao and Peng Yue" explains that Wei Bao left the Han alliance because he was upset with Liu Bang's "arrogance" and treatment of subordinates. In other chapters, Wei Bao is said to have deserted the Han ruler because of political calculation, a "rebellious and cunning temperament," or a misunderstanding of a prophecy that his own wife would produce a future emperor.[22] Why so many versions, we might ask? Can't Sima Qian simply decide which account of Wei Bao's motives is the most accurate one and omit the others—as Thucydides would have done?

The answers to these questions help explain the difference between the Chinese and the Western understandings of the purpose of history. Like Thucydides, Sima Qian tried to reflect accurately what he found in his sources. Yet he tried to be both "honest *and* generous" and used a principle of "concealing *and yet* revealing." This means that, in the case of Wei Bao, for example, the reason for his desertion from the Han alliance is presented more positively in the biographical chapter devoted to Wei Bao than it is elsewhere. Besides, since there were different explanations of this event in different sources, why not include all of them, thereby keeping open the possibility of doing justice to someone who may have been misunderstood and allowing the reader to make up his or her own mind? The use of inconsistent stories also allowed Sima Qian to engage in indirect criticism. Notice that Liu Bang is described positively only in his own "Annals" but is gently criticized in the "Biographies of Wei Bao and Peng Yue." If a person was clearly rather despicable, as was Empress Lü, one of Liu Bang's wives and the mother of his successor, it was important to make that clear. However, it was also important to Sima Qian to note that, despite her "lurid crimes," there was peace and prosperity when she was regent for her son.[23]

In evaluating Sima Qian, we must remember that, as a Confucian, he believed that humans were good by nature, even though their behavior did not always show it. Furthermore, humans were inconsistent in their goodness, often good in fits and starts. Today, we expect our histories to be unified and consistent chronological narratives which do not "jump around." We want our stories to move in a straight line. The Chinese, on the other hand, seem able to enter a story, like a room, in many ways, through many doors, moving first through the door which strikes them as most pleasing.

Perhaps it is easier to find goodness that way. Some scholars have contrasted this Chinese emphasis on "aesthetic order" with the "rational and logical order" found in Western thinking.[24] This way of organizing the past, with its awareness of the complexity of politics and human behavior, reflected Sima Qian's understanding of human beings, and it became the standard method used in all Chinese dynastic histories written from his day to the twentieth century.[25]

Whatever Sima Qian's *Records* lacks in chronological consistency it makes up for in the liveliness of his stories. In his collective biographies of assassins, Sima Qian described the attempt of one Jing Ke, who was hired by the crown prince to kill King Zheng of Qin (who had not yet become the famous First Emperor) with a poisoned dagger. The dagger was hidden in a map presented to the king by Jing Ke and, as the map was unrolled, the assassin grabbed the king's sleeve with his left hand and the dagger with his right, intending to stab the king quickly. However, Zheng pulled away, tearing his sleeve in the process. The ruler then ran around the room, trying to pull his sword which was stuck in its scabbard, while Jing Ke pursued him. When the king finally freed his sword, he struck Jing Ke, who had meanwhile thrown the dagger at the king and missed. The scene ended with a wounded Jing Ke, realizing he has failed, leaning on a pillar, laughing and cursing as he sprawled to the floor, awaiting his death at the hands of King Zheng's guards. Sima Qian's biography of Meng Tian, the chief builder of the fortifications in the north against the nomads, told readers that Meng Tian was marked for execution by the Legalist Zhao Gao, the scheming advisor to the second Qin emperor. Meng Tian told his executioners, before he swallowed poison, that he deserved death because, in building the wall in the north, he had committed the crime of "cutting through the earth's arteries." In his final paragraph, Sima Qian noted that the real reason he deserved death, if he did, was because he had not tried to "remedy the distresses of the people, minister to the old and enable the orphans to survive [nor did he] strive to cultivate harmony among the masses. Instead he embarked on great enterprises to pander to imperial ambition."[26] This was a proper Confucian judgment of the Qin official.

Many of Sima Qian's moral judgments come at the end of these biographies, in a paragraph which begins "The Grand Historian remarks. . . ." Seventy of the 130 chapters in the *Records* are biographies, either individual or collective. He recorded the lives of individual ministers, rebels, and rulers, as well as writing composite chapters on "Assassins," "Wandering Knights," "Good Officials," and "Harsh Officials." Indeed, according to a modern scholar, Sima Qian was a pioneer in "conceiving the idea that the life of individuals as well as that of the state or the age is a fit subject for the concentrated attention of the historian." As we have seen, the men and women (yes, he wrote about women as well, both the evil and the exemplary ones) were lively figures, designed to capture the attention of his readers so they would see the "profound and unchanging moral patterns that underlie the course of human events."[27]

However, not all of Sima Qian's stories, as we have seen, end with the proper Confucian moral. Sometimes, we are allowed to sympathize with, or at least understand, the behavior of rebellious servants, brutal women, and even assassins. One biographer argues that Sima Qian's life was marked by the tension between his desire for proper Confucian order and coherence (*li*) and his desire to be a good storyteller who appreciated the literature of the past (*wen*), whether it carried a Confucian message or not. We are told that Sima Qian's father, Sima Tan, was a man who appreciated Daoism as well as Confucianism. Since Daoism was not in favor at the court of the Emperor Wu, Sima Qian's employer, it is understandable that this official historian would depict his father as a man who, on his deathbed, urged his son to preserve the great deeds of the past so that Confucian values would be passed on. This need to carry out his filial duty to his father also explains why Sima Qian accepted castration—and legitimizes that decision, which many would otherwise look upon as cowardly.[28]

In the final analysis, Sima Qian may be the more psychologically interesting of these two ancient historians; his work is certainly the more complex. Yet each of these men reflected the values of his society. By writing truly memorable and exciting historical works, they were able to pass their basic questions—and some of the answers they gave to them—to later ages. Thucydides told one long, gripping story, which tried to analyze how the correct and incorrect use of political power contributed to the rise and fall of states. His moral lessons were directed to political leaders. Sima Qian told dozens of good stories and, in a different way than his Greek counterpart, used the past to teach individual moral lessons. Both captured readers, in their day and in ours, with stirring tales of greatness and despair, victory and defeat. The similarities between these two men and their histories show us what we have in common as human beings; the differences remind us how we can use the past to mirror our present values, even today.

Notes

1. Sima Qian, *Records of the Grand Historian,* trans. Burton Watson, *Han Dynasty I,* rev. ed. (New York: Columbia University Press, 1993),80.
2. *The Landmark Thucydides: A Comprehensive Guide to the Peloponnesian War,* ed. Robert B. Strassler (New York: Simon and Schuster, 1996), 3, 16.
3. Stephen W. Durrant, *The Cloudy Mirror: Tension and Conflict in the Writings of Sima Qian* (Albany: State University of New York Press, 1995), 8–9.
4. John H. Finley, Jr., *Thucydides* (Ann Arbor: University of Michigan Press, 1942), 9; *Landmark Thucydides,* ix–x.
5. Burton Watson, *Ssu-Ma Ch'ien: Grand Historian of China* (New York: Columbia University Press, 1958), 8–10, 35, 42–67.
6. Sima Qian, *Historical Records,* trans. Raymond Dawson (New York: Oxford University Press, 1994), xv–xvii.
7. See chapter 3 in this volume for an explanation of the ideas of Confucius.
8. See *Landmark Thucydides,* 577–596, for a good account of the political system in each city at the time of the war.
9. Ibid., 118.
10. Ibid., 112–117.
11. Ibid., 123–127.
12. Ibid., 128, 370–373.
13. Ibid., 477–478.
14. See Ibid., Book Eight, for an account of the events of the war from the defeat in Sicily to 411 B.C.E., when the narrative ends.
15. See Peter R. Pouncey, *The Necessities of War. A Study of Thucydides' Pessimism* (New York: Columbia University Press, 1980), ix–xiii; Lowell Edmunds, *Chance and Intelligence in Thucydides* (Cambridge: Harvard University Press, 1975), 213; A. Geoffrey Woodhead, *Thucydides on the Nature of Power* (Cambridge: Harvard University Press, 1970), 9, 20.
16. Although Thucydides stopped his narrative at the year 411 B.C.E. and didn't describe the final years of the war, he continued making additions to the text until his death, probably in 402 B.C.E. For an analysis of what parts of the *History* were written when, see Dennis Proctor, *The Experience of Thucydides* (Warminster, Eng.: Aris and Phelps, Ltd., 1980), 216–217.
17. Thucydides, *History of the Peloponnesian War,* trans. Rex Warner (New York: Penguin Books, 1954), 242.

18. *Landmark Thucydides*, 126, 200–201.
19. Sima Qian, *Records*, 77.
20. John E. Wills, Jr., *Mountain of Fame. Portraits in Chinese History* (Princeton: Princeton University Press, 1994), 63; Watson, *Ssu-ma Ch'ien*, 101–134.
21. Wills, *Mountain of Fame*, 64.
22. Sima Qian, *Records*, 69, 148; Grant Hardy, "Can an Ancient Chinese Historian Contribute to Modern Western Theory? The Multiple Narratives of Ssu-ma Ch'ien," *History and Theory*, vol. 33, no. 1 (1994): 26–31.
23. Watson, *Ssu-ma Ch'ien*, 95–97; Sima Qian, *Records*, 267–284.
24. See David Hall and Roger Ames, *Through Confucius* (Albany: State University of New York Press, 1987), discussed in Durrant, *The Cloudy Mirror*, 124.
25. Wills, *Mountain of Fame*, 64.
26. Sima Qian, *Historical Records*, 20–21, 55–61.
27. Watson, *Ssu-ma Ch'ien*, 124–126, 129.
28. Durrant, *The Cloudy Mirror*, xi–xviii, 1–27.

Further Reading

SIMA QIAN, *Historical Records*, trans. Raymond Dawson. New York: Oxford University Press, 1994. Contains material dealing with the ever-exciting Qin dynasty.

STRASSLER, ROBERT B., ed. *The Landmark Thucydides: A Comprehensive Guide to the Peloponnesian War*. New York: Free Press, 1996. The best way to read Thucydides; the translation is good, there are wonderful maps, and eleven essays at the end provide context.

WILLS, JOHN E., JR. *Mountains of Fame: Portraits in Chinese History*. Princeton: Princeton University Press, 1994. Contains good brief essay on Sima Qian on pp. 51–71.

CHAPTER 6

Asoka and Shi Huangdi: Honey and Vinegar

Is it more effective to govern people by moral persuasion or by coercion? Can the carrot be effective without the stick?

We have all heard it said that honey catches more flies than vinegar. If instead of trying to catch flies you are trying to govern a large kingdom, the question of whether to use force or gentleness, harsh laws or ethical persuasion, can be an important one.

The Buddhist emperor of India, Asoka Maurya (291–232 B.C.E.) inherited a large, diverse kingdom and attempted—with some success—to use a "law of piety" to hold it together. Asoka's Chinese contemporary, Shi Huangdi (259–210 B.C.E.), on the other hand, created a Chinese empire by consciously rejecting the moral standards for rulers prevalent in his day; he adopted the harsh practice of destroying all his enemies before they had a chance to destroy him. Both men were hard-working and self-confident. Asoka's empire crumbled within fifty years of his death, but he was remembered fondly by historians, especially Buddhist ones. Shi Huangdi, reviled by later Confucian historians, laid the foundations of an empire that lasted under various dynasties for over two thousand years. A look at the respective careers of these men will allow us to evaluate two different methods of government, and the different Asian societies that made each man's style of rule not only possible but maybe even sensible.

Asoka's empire was centered in the part of northeastern India known as Magadha, but his power spread from Kabul in the northwest as far east as modern Bangladesh and as far south as the city of Madras. This Mauryan Empire provided the Indian subcontinent with greater political unity than it was to have until modern times. It was founded by Asoka's grandfather, Chandragupta (ruled

322–299 B.C.E.), aided by his hard-nosed political advisor, Kautilya. Although Asoka came to the throne in 273 B.C.E. after the death of his father, Bindusara, he was not formally crowned until 269. It took him that long to seize full power from his brothers. Buddhist sources claim he killed between six and ninety-nine of them, the larger number doubtless an exaggeration.

The cultural, social, and economic vitality and diversity of third-century India, when combined with the strong central government provided by the Mauryan rulers, made India one of very few strong civilizations at that time. In the West, only the empire of Alexander the Great rivaled it.

Cultural diversity in India was aided by the relatively "new" religions of Buddhism and Jainism. Both rejected the strict Hindu caste system which placed humans into four principal groups: priests, warriors, traders and merchants, and laborers. These religions also rejected the ritual rules and the power of the Brahmins, or Hindu priests. As noted in an earlier chapter, the Buddha (560–480 B.C.E.) accepted Hindu ideas of moral cause and effect (karma) and of rebirth but simplified Hinduism by arguing that suffering and pain were caused by desire, which itself was caused by ignorance of spiritual truth. The Buddha's Noble Eightfold Path (right or correct views, aspirations, speech, conduct, livelihood, effort, mindfulness, and meditation) would lead the believer beyond suffering to Enlightenment, or salvation. This was the Buddhist path of duty or piety (dharma). We have also seen that Jains followed the teachings of another sixth-century reformer, the Mahavira (540–468 B.C.E.), who preached a stricter doctrine of non-violence to all living things than did Buddhists. They also believed that salvation could be achieved by a life of strict self-denial that would free the soul from all attachment to the physical world. After his conversion to Buddhism about ten years after his coronation, Asoka's edicts preaching dharma to his people showed the influence of all three major Indian religious traditions.

Social and economic diversity in the Indian subcontinent in Asoka's day was caused not only by the racial and linguistic variety that we still see in India, but also by the system of castes and subcastes that existed throughout the empire. Because the caste system was an essential part of Hinduism, as the population grew, members of the caste of merchants and traders were subdivided into hundreds of sub-categories, based upon place of residence, occupation, and family membership. People were not allowed to marry outside their caste. In short, there was a place for everyone and everyone was expected to stay in his or her place. After all, the reward for a good and stable life would be rebirth into a higher caste. This traditional Brahmanic teaching was being challenged in this period by Buddhist and Jain teachers but also by the growing economic and political powers of the merchants. Mauryan merchants traded extensively with both the Greek west and within the large empire. There was a thriving money economy, and merchant guilds often assumed political responsibilities. They raised groups of soldiers for self-protection, built public buildings, controlled wages and prices, and were received at court. Merchants brought taxes and wealth to the empire and were strongly supported by the Mauryan rulers.

This, then, was Asoka's world, the one to which he addressed his famous short sermons on morality and "piety." Those of Asoka's famous "edicts" that remain are described by the surface on which they were carved: fourteen Rock Edicts were carved on rocks along roadways, at least ten Pillar Edicts were "written" on tall pillars in population centers, and a few Cave Edicts were inscribed on the walls of caves, primarily for the inspiration of Buddhist monks. In an age without libraries and electronic mass media, this was an effective way to communicate. Tradition tells us that the king, referred to in the edicts as "Beloved of the Gods," was converted to Buddhism after a particularly bloody battle against the Kalinga people in the southeastern part of his empire. In this battle, fought in 262 B.C.E., about one hundred thousand were slain and at least that many deported. While Asoka was a follower of Buddhism before the Kalinga War, this conflict inspired a change of heart in the king. From this time until his death, Asoka actively preached dharma to his people through edicts and tours throughout his lands; he never again engaged in a major military campaign.

Before we consign this active monarch to the realm of pious legend as a remorseful but royal monk (as many Buddhist sources do) or write him off as a cynic who used religion, we need to look more closely at the nature of his dharma. The word *dharma* is difficult to translate and the concept difficult to understand. Words such as *piety, duty,* and *morality,* often used to translate dharma, suggest to many of us a fixed code of beliefs or practices for which an individual can be made strictly accountable. The Sanskrit word *dharma* refers to the duties demanded by one's station in life. While this varies for each caste, dharma requires all persons to treat others, especially family, with love and respect; to avoid the things which all men and women generally regard as evil, such as anger, cruelty, envy, and pride; and to seek out that which is good—love, truth, and beauty. It is important to understand that Asoka's concept of dharma was not specifically Hindu, Buddhist, or Jain. For a Hindu, especially one in the priestly caste, following dharma would require the performance of certain rituals; for many Buddhists, it involved certain monastic obligations. Beyond encouraging general ethical behavior (the king "desires security, self-control, impartiality, and cheerfulness for all living creatures"), Asoka's injunctions to his people were vague and ecumenical, showing the influence of all major Indian traditions. "Dharma is good," he wrote in Pillar Edict II, "but what does Dharma consist of? It consists of a few sins and many good deeds, of kindness, liberality, truthfulness, and purity." Who could argue with the wisdom of this? These words might help a Hindu be a better Hindu or a Buddhist be a more devout follower of the Noble Eightfold Path. And that, in the words of Rock Edict XII, is what the king wanted: "the promotion of each man's particular faith and the glorification of Dharma."[1]

King Asoka wished his subjects to be moral, but he allowed each to define the details of his or her own morality. After the midpoint of his reign, he genuinely believed that "all men are my children" and as such are capable of being trained and persuaded to live a good life. This required hard work, and Asoka set an example. He was a "morning person," rising early and engaging in prayers and meetings with the household staff before dealing with broader financial and military affairs. Breakfast at nine was followed by meetings with his council of ministers and reports from his agents. Some agents were dharma-mahamatas, or "morality ministers," who worked to see that the poor were not mistreated and that the affairs of the various religious communities were handled correctly. Asoka also built "rest stops" for weary travelers, dug wells, and kept roads in repair.

But, if Asoka wished his people to be moral and reasonably comfortable, he also wanted them to continue paying taxes. He may have been a missionary, but he was not naive. In one edict, the "Beloved of the Gods" invited even the "forest people" in the remote sections of his domains "to adopt this way of life and this ideal." He reminded them, however, "that he exercises the power to punish, despite his repentance, in order to induce them to desist from their crimes."[2] Asoka's Buddhist and Jain-inspired dislike of violence never resulted in a lifting of the death penalty. His attempt to create a "national" or "imperial" morality, while a product of genuine conviction, was also a shrewd way for the monarch to centralize imperial authority in a large, culturally diverse empire. Religious toleration can be virtuous; it can also be good politics when one's empire contains dozens of different and competing sects. Kautilya, the hard-headed political realist who had helped Chandragupta create the Mauryan empire, would have found much to commend in Asoka's policy. Even the strong Buddhist flavor of Asoka's dharma was attractive to the commercial classes, who desired a moral alternative to Hindu caste restrictions. Asoka's emphasis on non-violence appealed to the Jains, while his acceptance (though not necessarily encouragement) of caste practices avoided giving offense to the Hindus. In promoting this broad but still very Indian ethical code, Asoka, in the words of one scholar, "was attempting to reform the narrow attitude of religious teaching to protect the weak against the strong, and to promote throughout the empire a consciousness of social behavior so broad in its scope that no cultural group could object to it."[3]

Protecting the weak against the strong was the least of the worries of King Zheng of Qin [the dynasty is pronounced "chin" and Shi Huangdi was a title meaning First Emperor], the man who created a Chinese empire out of seven warring states in 221 B.C.E. Despite his great achievement, King Zheng remains an awesome, controversial, and somewhat mysterious figure. The history of his reign by historian Sima Qian, who wrote at the beginning of the first century B.C.E., describes this King of Qin as having "a waspish nose, eyes like slits, a chicken breast, and a voice like a jackal. He is merciless, with the heart of a tiger or wolf."[4] The Sovereign Emperor was clearly a man to be reckoned with. Both friend and foe found him formidable—and that was the way he liked it.

After coming to the throne of Qin in 246 at the age of thirteen, it took King Zheng twenty-five years to conquer the other six kingdoms in the Yellow River valley and to unify China. King Zheng (then Shi Huangdi, or First Emperor) ruled over the unified Chinese empire for only eleven years until his death in 210, but his impact was profound and some still argue about the wisdom of his policies and the nature of his contribution to Chinese history. Chinese folktales lament the suffering caused by the building of the Great Wall and other imperial projects. It is understandable that a man strong enough to create an empire out of the feudal disorder that had plagued China for centuries might make a few enemies in the process. Yet this man can also be considered the father of his country. He laid the foundations for the later accomplishments of the Han dynasty (206 B.C.E. to 220 C.E.). Nonetheless, Shi Huangdi is almost universally condemned by Chinese historians. This animosity stems in part from the fact that they were Confucians and he was not. That he executed 460 Confucian scholars and sent others into exile after ordering all their texts burned may have also contributed to their dislike.

The roots of this conflict go back several centuries and require some review of the philosophy of Confucius, treated in chapter 3. Confucius (551–479 B.C.E.), a great master of ethical philosophy, emphasized a moral code based on *li* (propriety) and *jen* (humanity). By observing proper rituals and showing respect for parents and ancestors, one demonstrated self-control and self-respect. Confucius believed in authority, but he stressed the importance of virtuous behavior on the part of the ruler. If a leader practiced charity and good faith in dealing with his subjects, his kingdom would be well-governed. If all officials from the ruler to the local magistrate acted in accordance with the virtues of *li* and *jen,* the result would be order and obedience in the land. A later Confucian thinker, Mo Tzu (479–381 B.C.E.), went even further and argued that rulers should feed and clothe their people, avoid war altogether, and trust in the natural goodness of people to follow "the path of righteousness."

Education, especially one which stressed the values of the past and loyalty to the family, was important to these men. Scholarship was a path to virtue. Though this view of politics and morality would have been congenial to Asoka, it was alien to the rulers of the state of Qin, a "barbarian" frontier land. Barbarian or not, however, the rulers of Qin during the fourth century were quicker than their more civilized Chinese neighbors to end feudalism and create a strong central government, backed by a system of taxation and a powerful army. Without the family and feudal outbursts that kept other states in a condition of near-constant civil war, the Qin rulers were able to defeat the armies of the states of Han, Zhao, Wei, Yan, and Qi during the late fourth and early third centuries B.C.E. By the time Zheng became King of Qin in 246 B.C., his state was already the most powerful in the Yellow River valley and had rejected Confucian virtues of moderation and kindness in favor of the very different philosophy of Legalism.

At the Qin court, the Legalist ideas of Han Feizi, were advanced by Li Si, chief advisor to King Zheng and a guiding force behind many of his policies. They believed that harsh laws, speedily enforced, were more useful than moral example in securing obedience from subjects. They also suggested that troops were more effective than tedious Confucian rituals and etiquette. "Talent and wisdom," wrote Han Feizi, "are not sufficient to subdue the masses, but power and position are able to subject even men of talent." Legalists advocated what we would today call a strong, secular, amoral state. You can win by doing the things that your enemies would be ashamed to do, one Legalist text advised. Legalist philosophy and Qin ambition were made for each other. Li Si got a job and a chance to be a powerful man. The Qin ruler found someone who would tell him that killing several hundred soldiers after they surrendered was not really all that bad. Li Si advised his king to bribe the feudal lords of other states; "as for those who were unwilling, they would be stabbed with sharp swords" and the army sent to finish the job.[5]

Despite (or perhaps because of) his Legalist disdain for morality, Shi Huangdi's specific and lasting achievements were impressive. He turned China from a patchwork of squabbling kingdoms into a state governed from a central capital at Xian Yang. When King Zheng conquered a state, he sent the ruling family and others who might challenge his power to his capital—and sold their land. He also organized his realm into provinces and prefectures, or counties. The former were originally military districts, while the latter were administrative ones and used for purposes of tax collection. Eventually, civil and military leaders were placed in each province. Since these officials were not members of the emperor's family or of high noble rank (as they might have been under the old system), there was less chance they would try to challenge the emperor. Besides, placing a number of major officials in each of his thirty-six provinces almost guaranteed that they would quarrel with each other; this left final authority in the hands of the emperor.

Shi Huangdi's centralization extended to standardized weights and measures, the characters used to write the Chinese language (to allow officials to communicate with those who spoke dialects), and even the length of cart axles so that all carts could use the same tracks. The First Emperor also created the first civil service and paid officials in coin, not in land, out of the taxes they helped collect. There were no private armies during Shi Huangdi's reign, and the laws of the land were public, if very harsh. Finally, the new emperor built many roads, several hundred new palaces, and elaborate defensive fortifications in the north, known later as the Great Wall.

The latter building projects illustrates Shi Huangdi's extravagance. His Great Wall, which connected and strengthened existing fortifications, was needed to protect China from the nomadic tribes of Turks and Mongols, that periodically attacked and devastated Chinese cities. Whether China needed a gigantic wall with numerous watchtowers, however, is debatable. The nearly 1 million men who labored and died building it over twelve years would have probably disagreed. Nearly as many men, seven hundred thousand, spent thirty years building an elaborate tomb for the emperor at Mount Li, near Xian and the Yellow River. Part of the tomb consisted of a three-acre flat-roofed underground vault containing life-sized, individualized statues of an army of eight thousand men and horses, including full-scale bronze chariots and charioteers and images of all members of the emperor's family and household staff. While Shi Huangdi was not the first to construct an elaborate grave site (earlier, Shang dynasty rulers buried real people instead of statues), the magnitude of Shi Huangdi's effort helps us understand why some called him a megalomaniac.[6]

He also built 270 palaces near his capital, some of them replicas of those of his conquered enemies. These were justified for security reasons, since they allowed him to sleep in a different place every night. One precise and telling example of the emperor's arrogance is found in Sima Qian's history. On one occasion, a "great gale" prevented the ruler's ship from crossing the Yangtze River near the temple of Mount Xiang. In order to punish the local goddess, the Princess of the River Xiang, "the emperor in his rage made three thousand convicts cut down all the trees on Mount Xiang, leaving the mountain bare."[7] Clearly, this man took himself very seriously. He believed himself to be the first of a line of ten thousand emperors. Shi Huangdi's inscriptions did not urge men to live morally; they bragged that "his influence knows no end, his will is obeyed and his orders will remain through eternity."[8]

Of course, Shi Huangdi's enemies and their ideas did outlive him. By the end of the Qin dynasty in 206 B.C.E., the philosophy of Legalism was thoroughly discredited by the excesses of Shi Huangdi and his son. Both Han Feizi and Li Si died violent deaths. It was fitting that the first of the rebellions that broke out after Shi Huangdi's death was led by two farmers who were late in reporting for forced labor on one of the imperial projects. Since the penalty for being late was immediate execution, they decided their chances of survival would be better if they started a revolt. It was the first of many that led to the collapse of the Qin empire. Had the law been less stringent, this revolt may not have started.

Confucian historians quickly made this point, beginning with the famous essay on "The Faults of Qin," written by Han dynasty poet and statesman Jia Yi (201–169 B.C.E.). He remarked on the military skill of Qin generals but then asked why such a feared dynasty could be overthrown with such relative ease. Jia's answer has echoed through twenty centuries of Chinese history: "Because it failed to rule with humanity and righteousness and to realize that the power to attack and the power to retain what one has won are not the same."[9] The general verdict was that Shi Huangdi and his dynasty got what they deserved. We might note in passing Confucian historians insincerity and self-righteousness. None of them regretted Chinese unification, only the methods used to achieve it.

Perhaps the moral of this story, if there is one, is that both honey and vinegar are necessary. One historian of China has written that although "force can never give a permanent unity . . . its use may be necessary to establish this unity in the beginning." The accomplishments of the Han period would have been impossible without the achievements of the preceding Qin empire.[10] Asoka was both realistic and pious. He received better treatment from historians than did Shi Huangdi, but his empire survived him by only a few decades. At least Asoka did understand that force had its place but that some things simply cannot be forced. In one of his edicts, he noted that "people can be induced to advance in dharma by only two means, by moral prescriptions and by meditation." He confessed that morals were "of little consequence but meditation was of great importance . . . it is by meditation that people have progressed in Dharma most."[11]

Notes

1. *The Edicts of Asoka*, ed. and trans. N. A. Nikam and Richard McKeon (Chicago: University of Chicago Press, 1959), 41, 52.
2. Ibid., 28–29.
3. Romila Thapar, *Asoka and the Decline of the Mauryas* (Oxford: Oxford University Press, 1961), 181.
4. Li Yu-ning, ed., *The First Emperor of China* (White Plains, NY: International Arts and Sciences Press, 1975), 264.
5. Derk Bodde, *China's First Unifier: A Study of the Ch'in Dynasty as Seen in the Life of Li Si, 280–208 BC* (Hong Kong: Hong Kong University Press, 1967), 14–15, 189. (The name of the Qin dynasty and state is spelled Ch'in in all but the most recently published works.)
6. Audrey Topping, "China's Incredible Find," *National Geographic Magazine* (April 1978): 440–459; Audrey Topping, "Clay Soldiers: The Army of Emperor Chin," *Horizon* (January 1977): 2, 4–13.
7. Li Yu-ning, ed., *The First Emperor of China*, 275.
8. Ibid., 271–272.
9. Ibid., 281–282.
10. Bodde, *China's First Unifier*, 236–237.
11. *Edicts of Asoka*, 40.

Further Reading

Edicts of Asoka. Ed. and trans. N. A. NIKAM and RICHARD MCKEON. Chicago: University of Chicago Press, 1959. Sample Asoka's ideas directly.

GOKHALE, B. K. *Asoka Maurya*. New York: Twayne Publishers, 1966. Best short biography of Asoka.

TOPPING, AUDREY. "China's Incredible Find." *National Geographic Magazine* (April 1978): 440–459. The title is not an exaggeration; see for yourself.

WALEY, ARTHUR. *Three Ways of Thought in Ancient China*. London: Allen and Unwin, 1931. See the chapter on "The Realists" for a good description of Legalism.

CHAPTER 7

Boudica and Zenobia: Challenging the Romans

Why were Roman armies difficult to defeat? What makes female warriors attractive to historians?

There was a military "disaster" in Britain in 60–61 C.E. Celtic tribesmen led by Queen Boudica destroyed three Roman settlements, including Londinium (London), killing perhaps seventy thousand Romans before legionnaires were able to crush the "barbarian" army. In his description of these events, the Roman historian Cassius Dio wrote: "all this ruin was brought upon the Romans by a woman, a fact which in itself caused them the greatest shame."[1]

Just over two centuries later, from 267–271 C.E., another female ruler challenged the Romans. Zenobia, Arab queen of the city-state of Palmyra in Syria, conquered most of the eastern half of the Roman Empire, including Egypt, before being defeated and taken captive to Rome to march in Emperor Aurelian's victory procession.

Both of these female rulers presented serious political and military challenges to the Roman Empire; both were ambitious leaders who achieved dramatic successes but suffered even more dramatic failures in their attempts to defeat the Romans. The stories of these slightly mysterious women (we know when Boudica died but have neither her birth date nor the birth and death dates of Zenobia) can help us better understand why the Romans remained such a strong military power for so many centuries. In addition, although neither their victories nor their defeat had much to do with their gender, the way they were treated by historians helps us see what fascinates both ancient and modern writers about "warrior queens" who take up the sword in defense or in conquest.[2]

Of these two rulers, Queen Boudica (sometimes incorrectly called Boadicea) has received the greatest attention, since nineteenth-century Englishmen saw her as a heroine whose boldness in attacking Rome foreshadowed the patriotic spirit of the British empire of their day. Of course, Boudica's story tells us more about the ancient Britons and Romans than it does about modern Englishmen. And it begins, like many stories about Rome, with Julius Caesar.

In 55–54 B.C.E., Caesar, having subdued most of Gaul [modern France], decided to make a foray across the English Channel. He was able to temporarily occupy territory in southeastern Britain and made alliances with five tribes who saw the Romans as allies against a more powerful tribe, the Catuvellauni. Caesar left Britain in 54 B.C.E., leaving the island open to Roman trade and political influence but free of direct Roman military control. It was not until nearly a century later, in 43 C.E., that the Roman Emperor Claudius again brought troops across the English Channel, this time to stay. Disputes among various British groups again worked in favor of the Romans, and the Romans established allies in the form of client kings who would support Rome as a way of maintaining their independence in these tribal disputes.

One of these client kings was Prasutagus of the Iceni, a Celtic people located in what is today East Anglia, about 75 miles northeast of London. He was married to Boudica and it was his death in 60 C.E. that became the trigger for the Boudican revolt against Rome.[3]

In an effort to protect his lands, Prasutagus made a will in which he granted half of his kingdom to the Romans, hoping in this way to maintain the independence of the other half for his people and his family, headed by Boudica and their two daughters. The Romans had other ideas. They had never intended that the states of client kings like Pratsutagus should remain independent after the death of the ruler. Therefore, after Pratsutagus' death, the Roman procurator [chief financial administrator] arrived at Boudica's residence to make an inventory of all her lands and possessions and claim all of them for Rome. When Boudica objected, she was beaten "like a common criminal and her daughters, as spoils of war, were raped by all and sundry." The property of the leading Iceni families was also seized.[4]

The treatment of their queen might itself have been enough to trigger an uprising. Yet, there were additional reasons for British unhappiness. Some years earlier, the Romans had taken three actions that offended their native subjects. First, as was their practice, they settled some of their retired veteran soldiers on land taken from the British in and around the settlement of Camulodunum [modern city of Colchester]. On this "stolen" land, which had been the headquarters of a group known as the Trinovantes, allies of the Romans since the time of Caesar, the Romans added insult to injury by using British taxes to build a large temple to the Emperor Claudius, thus bringing an alien religious presence into the heart of a former British royal settlement. Second, prior to his movement further west in 48–49 C.E, the Roman governor Publius Ostorius Scapula decided to disarm the tribes in the southeast, even those, like the Iceni and the Trinovantes, who were Roman client states and saw themselves as allies. Finally, about six years prior to the death of Pratsugatus, Roman moneylenders began calling in loans that they had made to British leaders in the years just after the conquest in 43 C.E. The Britons had understood these to be gifts, not loans, and were naturally upset.[5]

The stage was now set for the revolt of Queen Boudica, a revolt that came within one battle of chasing the Romans out of Britain. At the time Boudica was being assaulted by the Roman procurator, the Roman military governor of Britain, Gaius Suetonius Paulinus, was about as far from the Icenian lands as he could get. He was attacking the Druid priests and their supporters on the island of Mona (now Anglesey) off the far western coast of Britain. This allowed Boudica to raise an army of over 100,000, primarily from her tribe and the Trinovantes.

Her first target was the Roman colony at Camulodunum. Since the colony was unprotected by a wall, it was easy for Boudica's troops to surround it and burn it to the ground. The retired veterans, aided by a mere 200 legionnaires sent from Londinium, were outnumbered and only able to gather themselves and women and children into the temple of Claudius to make a final defense. After two days the temple was burned and its inhabitants killed. The hated temple to the alien Roman god [by this time, Romans were claiming that emperors were divine] was destroyed and a statue of the Emperor Claudius beheaded. A relief force of about 2,000 Roman soldiers was ambushed and destroyed by the Britons before it could arrive at Camulodunum.[6]

As Boudica's troops were completing their plunder of Camulodunum, the Roman governor Suetonius was rushing back from defeating the Druids to meet this new threat. One historian pointed out that Boudica's men might have been able to ambush Suetonius as he was rushing back east as they had the earlier group of legionnaires heading toward Camulodunum. However, the Britons instead spent three days enjoying their earlier victory.[7] Had they defeated Suetonius at this point, the Romans would have been forced to leave Britain. When Suetonius arrived in Londinium and reviewed the situation, "he decided to sacrifice the single city of Londinium to save the province as a whole."[8] Those who were able left with the governor and his troops, but many of the old and infirm had no means of escape.

The Roman settlement at Londinium, although not as important as Camulodunum, was already an important center for merchants and trade; it covered thirty acres and had grown to 30,000 inhabitants when Suetonius decided to sacrifice it to Boudica's army.[9] And sacrifice it he did, as the Britons were easily able to capture it and burn it to the ground. Roman historian Tacitus reported quite concisely that inhabitants "were slaughtered by the enemy. . . . For the British did not take or sell prisoners, or practice other wartime exchanges. They could not wait to cut throats, hang, burn and crucify. . . ."[10] Archeologists investigating this event also found over 100 skulls cut from bodies and a red layer of soil sixteen inches deep resting thirteen feet below the surface of modern London. This is the substratum of debris burned in the attack by Boudica's troops.[11]

From London, Boudica turned her forces northwest toward the city of Verulamium [modern St. Albans], which may have been evacuated by the time her army got there. British tribesmen loyal to Rome were its principal inhabitants. It too was burned to the ground. In the three settlements combined, Boudica's army killed tens of thousands of Romans. Now it was the turn of Suetonius and the Romans to respond.

Boudica's army had grown to over 100,000 as a result of her victories, but it was not as large as the 250,000 men reported by the dramatic Dio Cassius. Since Suetonius had many fewer men, perhaps only 7,000 to 8,000, it was important that he find a place to fight the Britons where the terrain would be to his advantage. He therefore let Boudica chase him northwest until he found a spot where he could position his legionnaires with their backs to a forest so that they could not be surrounded by the much larger British army. He also placed his troops behind a river and in a narrow area that would make it difficult for Boudica's men to maneuver.

Since the Romans were still outnumbered at least ten to one, the key to their victory was their equipment and their disciplined fighting tactics. Boudica's army was huge but not well-trained. The men had brought wagons with supplies and with many family members who came to watch the glorious victory against Rome. These wagons, arrayed behind the army, would later block their escape as the Romans pushed forward. The Romans began the battle by unleashing thousands of javelins at a distance of forty yards from the British forces. Since the British had no breastplates or other armor, many were killed in this initial onslaught. Although there were still many more Britons than Romans on the battlefield, Boudica's men began to retreat, allowing the Romans, marching in precision behind their shields, to divide the enemy into smaller groups which could be killed by sword and arrows. Although it took nearly four hours of desperate fighting by both sides, the Romans finally had their revenge as the Britons either fled or were eventually isolated and killed. Women, children, and pack animals were killed as well. In the words of a modern author, "the Romans must have gone mad with blood lust." Boudica apparently poisoned herself and her daughters at the end of the battle, in which Tacitus tells us 80,000 Britons and only 400 Romans were killed. Following the defeat of Boudica and the remnants of her forces over the following months, the Romans, according to Tacitus, sent in a new governor who "governed the province with a certain gentleness of administration" while the British came to admire certain "attractive vices" of the Romans when they were able to take time from their own civil wars to do so.[12] Perhaps Boudica's response to her ill treatment had taught the Romans a political lesson just as the Roman legions had taught the British a military one.

There was little the Romans could learn from our second challenger to Roman authority, Queen Septimia Zenobia, ruler of the Roman colony of Palmyra. She was a wiser, more cynical, and shrewder opponent of Rome than Boudica. With considerably stronger forces than those available to the British queen, Zenobia "embarked on one of the most remarkable challenges to the sovereignty of Rome that had been seen. . . ."[13] Yet in the end she too was a victim of Roman military skill.

Located in what is today west central Syria midway between Damascus and the Euphrates River, Palmyra was an important trading center on the caravan route between Rome and central Asia. Palmyra's wealthy independent merchants traded with Phoenicia and Egypt as well as with central and east Asia. It became part of the Roman Empire in 114 C.E. and was famous for its skilled archers who helped the Romans protect their eastern frontier against the Parthians. Because of its importance, Rome treated the city's inhabitants with respect, allowing them to collect their own taxes so long as they remained loyal. When Parthia was conquered by a much stronger Sassanid Persian empire in 227 C.E., Palmyran friendship became much more important to the Romans. In 230 C.E. members of the Palmyran royal family were made Roman senators, and leading citizens of Palmyra began to adopt Roman names.[14]

Palmyra's loyalty to Rome was tested in 260 C.E. when the Persians defeated, held captive, and eventually killed the Roman Emperor Valerian. Zenobia's husband, the Palmyran ruler Odainat (Odaenathus in Latin), who had been honored by the Romans by being made a Roman Consul in 258, took the field, defeating both the Persians and a local claimant to Roman rule in Syria in 261. In return for this, the Roman Emperor Gallienus gave him the title of *"dux Romanorum,"* or "leader of the Romans." It was important, to the Romans at least, that Odainat was not given the title "Augustus" or Emperor, a title that Zenobia would later claim.[15] He was special, but not that special.

Zenobia's story really begins in 267 after her husband and stepson were assassinated and she became the regent [acting ruler] on behalf of her own son Wahballat (Vaballathus in Latin). Since the Romans were busy at this time fighting the Goths in Europe, Zenobia decided the time was right make a change in Palmyra's "foreign policy." She sent an army into Egypt to attack a usurper to Roman rule. Although she claimed to be acting on behalf of Rome, as Odainat had done, it was soon clear that she was acting in her own behalf and that of her son. After the Egyptian campaign, she claimed land north of Egypt, including most of Asia Minor [modern Turkey] nearly as far as the city of Byzantium.

During her four years as ruler of her short-lived Palmyran Empire, Zenobia used the wealth of her city freely. She invited the Greek scholar Cassius Longinus to Palmyra to lend intellectual brilliance to her court. She encouraged religious tolerance and spent lavishly on expensive jewelry for herself and her courtiers. She spoke Egyptian and claimed the famous Queen Cleopatra as her ancestor. One modern historian said that Zenobia was dominated by a "fierce, insatiable ambition."[16] By 271, she controlled the eastern third of the Roman Empire. Especially important was the Roman grain supply, most of which by this time came from Egypt. In 271 she also had coins minted with her son's image and the title of Augustus and without the image of the Roman Emperor Aurelian.[17]

These were clear challenges to Roman authority that Emperor Aurelian, fresh from victory over the Goths in the north, could not ignore. He led a large Roman army into Asia Minor heading toward Palestine. Just outside Antioch on the Orontes River, Zenobia awaited him with an army of 70,000 men. Aurelian, aware of the power of the heavily armed and self-confident Palmyran cavalry, told his own troops to flee from them, luring them on until, in the words of an ancient historian, both men and horses were "thoroughly tired through the excessive heat and weight of their armour."[18] At that point, the Romans turned and had an easy time defeating the weakened Palmyran horsemen. The rest of the Palmyran army fled toward the city of Antioch, which only agreed to admit them because Zenobia's general Zabdas tricked leaders of the city by dressing up one of his soldiers to look like the Emperor Aurelian, whom he claimed to have captured.[19]

During the night, Zenobia and her diminished army slipped out of Antioch and headed east toward the city of Emesa. Here the Palmyran cavalry successfully charged their Roman counterparts, inflicting heavy casualties on the Romans. However, the Roman infantry was also to take advantage of a break in the line of Zenobia's infantry and eventually scattered her troops. Zenobia again retreated, this time to her home city of Palmyra.[20] Aurelian's army of 40,000 men pursued her, carrying elaborate siege machines with them on a three-day march through the Syrian Desert. Because of the clear determination of the Romans to carry on a long siege, some of Zenobia's allies deserted her. In a desperate attempt to secure help from the Persians, she slipped out of Palmyra and headed by fast camel toward the Euphrates River. Unable to find a boat to take her across quickly, she fell into Romans hands. Palmyra opened its gates to the Romans when they heard of her capture, and Zenobia and the leading members of her court, including General Zabdas and Longinus, were taken to Emesa for trial. According to one account, Zenobia then took refuge in her status as a member of the "weaker sex," blaming her action on bad advice given her by Longinus, Zabdas, and others.[21]

While this last episode in Zenobia's story may or may not be true, we do know that Longinus and others were executed and Zenobia was taken to Rome, where she was paraded in her golden jewelry as part of Aurelian's traditional Roman triumphal parade through the city. Zenobia apparently ended her life some years later at a villa in the city of Tibur (modern Tivoli) as the wife of a Roman senator. She never returned to her home city, which was attacked and left in ruins by the Romans following a second revolt just a year after Zenobia's capture.

It is important to remember that these two "warrior queens" were no more successful than many dozens, even hundreds, of European and Asian leaders who contested Roman rule during the 700-year history of the Roman Republic and Empire. Because it was a highly trained force, able to fight together in close order behind protective shields and breastplates, the Roman infantry was able to defeat larger but less well-trained armies. The final battle against Boudica is a classic example of the patience and discipline of the Roman foot soldiers. When the Romans fought other professional armies, such as those of Palmyra, Roman commanders had to use their judgment and tactical skills to outwit their enemies. This ability served the emperor Aurelian very well in dealing with Zenobia's army. He was a skilled soldier in a century when most Roman rulers were military men with considerable field experience. Even before the "soldier-emperors" of the third century, the Romans were a people with a strong military ethos. After all, they were nearly always fighting someone, somewhere. Years of peace were rare. The Romans also learned much from the Greeks, who invented the phalanx, a square infantry formation that moved together, something like a human tank, and from others who had defeated them on occasion, such as Hannibal and the Carthaginians during the second Punic War.

The Roman Empire did not finally collapse in the west during the fifth century because Romans lacked military skill. Rome fell for a host of reasons, many of them social and economic. Among other things, Rome no longer had sufficient tax money to pay soldiers or to defend its northern frontier. The fate of Boudica and Zenobia was repeated many times during the history of the Roman Empire, although generally it was men who played the leading roles in these dramas.

Boudica and Zenobia capture our attention, and that of ancient and modern historians, because they were women. Both ancient and modern writers have ambivalent feelings about these "warrior queens." They admire their courage, especially in the case of Boudica, and their beauty and intelligence, especially in the case of Zenobia, yet cannot resist, in some cases, making statements about these females that reflect the historian's own bias. Ancient historians had no qualms about telling us what their characters "would have" said, especially if this would result in a better story.

Both of these tendencies, especially the penchant for "elaboration," are especially clear in the writing about Boudica. All the written information we have about this person comes from two Roman historians, Dio Cassius and Cornelius Tacitus. Dio has Boudica deliver an extensive speech to her assembled army before launching her campaign against Rome. After introducing the queen as a woman "possessed of greater intelligence than often belongs to women," Dio describes her as "very tall, in appearance most terrifying, in the glance of her eye most fierce," and possessed of a "harsh" voice. Her "great mass of the tawniest [sandy colored] hair fell to her hips" as she addressed her troops, exhorting them to live as free men instead of slaves and telling them that they were braver than the Romans because they fought without body armor and were not "soft" like their enemy: "they [Romans] require shade and covering, they require kneaded bread and wine and oil, and if any of these things fail them, they perish; for us, on the other hand, any grass or root serves as bread, the juice of any plant as oil, any water as wine, any tree as a house."[22]

While the second ancient historian of Boudica, Tacitus, is more modest, he too has her deliver a speech on the eve of her final battle with the Romans. It deserves to be quoted in full since it tells us as much about the historian as it does about his subject.

> "We British are used to women commanders in war," she cried. "I am descended from mighty men! But I am not fighting for my kingdom and wealth now. I am fighting as an ordinary person for my lost freedom, my bruised body, and my outraged daughters. Nowadays Roman rapacity does not even spare our bodies. Old people are killed, virgins raped. But the gods will grant us the vengeance we deserve! The Roman division which dared to fight is annihilated. The others cower in their camps, or watch for a chance to escape. They will never face even the din and roar of all

our thousands, much less the shock of our onslaught. Consider how many of you are fighting—and why! Then you will win this battle, or perish. That is what I, a women, plan to do!—let the men live in slavery if they will."[23]

Both of these authors contrasted the sometimes noble but "primitive" Britons with the more sophisticated Romans. Dio Cassius, despite his attempt to make his British queen into a classical orator, complete with stirring language and measured phrases, does provide some balance in his account since he also includes a speech given before the final battle by the Roman general in which Suetonius appeals to Roman pride, reminds his soldiers of the earlier British brutalities, and warns them that they had better win or perish since they were fighting "wild beasts" who would kill them as horribly as they had the Romans in Camulodunum. For his part, Tacitus is more interested than Dio in reminding his Roman readers that Rome shared some of the blame for the disaster in Britain. Since his father-in-law, Agricola, was an official serving under Suetonius at the time of the Boudican Revolt, Tacitus likely had accurate, first-hand information on the situation at that time. In his *Agricola,* he does not mince words in criticizing his countrymen. "They, the Britons, had country, wives, parents as reasons for war, the Romans had avarice and luxury."[24] His account of the actual war is brief and matter-of-fact in tone, with none of the dramatic or gruesome details that Dio, writing later, would supply. Interestingly, neither Roman writer makes very much of the fact that Boudica was female. Tacitus does not even bother to suggest that she was more intelligent than most women, a comment Dio's readers doubtless read without any sense of either amusement or outrage.

When historians evaluate Zenobia, the picture is somewhat different. She must have been a very attractive woman, since writers both ancient and modern comment on this fact. Authors writing in the century after her death referred to her as "most beautiful" and "of an incredible attraction." She was reputed to have "powerful black eyes, teeth white as pearls and a wonderful dark complexion." Her name in Arabic, Al-Zabba, is said to mean "one with beautiful long hair."[25] Historians also praised Zenobia for her masculine courage. She hunted with her husband and drank with her generals, it was said, but was "chaste," at least to the point of only sleeping with her husband in order to have children. As part of this idealized picture, her voice was reported to be clear and command-ing, not harsh like that of Boudica.[26]

Zenobia is remembered as glamorous, but also as ambitious and not particularly admirable. She was, one modern scholar pointed out, "a ruthless woman" who "sacrificed to her personal ambitions the fortune of her native city, which Odaenathus had by his loyalty to the Empire preserved."[27] Another wrote that "unlike Boudica, Zenobia had not been wronged: she had not been scourged, her daughters had not been raped, the Romans had not taken over her people's land nor imposed lethal taxes upon Palmyra."[28]

So Boudica, while unsophisticated in the eyes of Roman histori-ans, at least has some nobility; her courage in defending her land was a virtue Tacitus would want his fellow Romans to imitate. Zenobia was beautiful and colorful, but also greedy and ambitious. What is important, then, is not that these women fought the Ro-mans. What is important is that, of the many people who did fight the Romans over the long expanse of Roman history, these two leaders were significant enough in the eyes of their contemporaries that they became part of the historical record. Were they remem-bered because female warriors were so rare—in their day and ours? Or were they remembered because their courage shames or threat-ens male leadership in our still patriarchal society? Is this why male historians often see such women as both beautiful and ruthless, in-triguing but also evil? Perhaps these questions, like the mystery that still surrounds Boudica and Zenobia, are best left to the psychologists.

Notes

1. *Dio's Roman History*, VIII, trans by Earnest Cary (Cambridge: Harvard University Press, 1925), 83.
2. See Antonia Fraser, *The Warrior Queens: The Legends and the Lives of the Women Who Have Led Their Nations in War* (New York: Random House Vintage, 1990), especially 3–13 and 323–335, for a fuller discussion of the concept of the "warrior queen" using Boudica as her model.
3. The best account of the Boudican revolt is Graham Webster, *Boudica, The British Revolt Against Rome AD 60* (London: Routledge, 1978; re-vised edition, 1993). A good shorter account is found in Michael Wood, *In Search of the Dark Ages* (British Broadcasting Company, 1981), 13–37.

4. Webster, *Boudica*, 88.
5. Webster, *Boudica*, 58–62, 83–84; *Dio's Roman History*, VIII, 83.
6. Webster, *Boudica*, 90–91.
7. Fraser, *Warrior Queens*, 79.
8. Tacitus, *Annals of Imperial Rome* (London: Penguin, 1956), 319.
9. Fraser, *Warrior Queens*, 80–81.
10. Tacitus, *Annals*, 319.
11. Fraser, *Warrior Queens*, 84–85.
12. Michael Wood, *In Search of the Dark Ages*, 32; Tacitus, *Annals*, 319–320; Tacitus, *Agricola*, (Indianapolis: Bobbs-Merrill, 1967), 14. The fullest ancient account of the battle is in *Dio's Roman History*, VIII, 103.
13. Richard Stoneman, *Palmyra and its Empire: Zenobia's Revolt Against Rome* (Ann Arbor: University of Michigan Press, 1992), 155.
14. Fraser, *Warrior Queens*, 111–113.
15. Fraser, *Warrior Queens*, 114.
16. Fraser, *Warrior Queens*, 119.
17. Stoneman, *Palmyra*, 159–160; see also Philip Walsingham Sergeant, *Dominant Women* (Freeport, NY: Books for Libraries Press, 1969), 68–71.
18. Fraser, *Warrior Queens*, 122, quoting the ancient historian Zosimus.
19. Stoneman, *Palmyra*, 170, relying upon Zosimus.
20. Stoneman, *Palmyra*, 171, citing Zosimus as his source.
21. Stoneman, *Palmyra*, 176–77; Fraser, *Warrior Queens*, 124.
22. *Dio's Roman History*, VIII, 85–91.
23. Tacitus, *Annals*, 320.
24. *Dio's Roman History*, VIII, 97–101; Tacitus, *Agricola*, 13.
25. Fraser, *Warrior Queens*, 114; Stoneman, *Palmyra*, 111.
26. Fraser, *Warrior Queens*, 114–115.
27. Arnold Hugh Martin Jones, *The Oxford Classical Dictionary*, Second Edition, edited by N. G. Hammond and H. H. Scullard (Oxford: Oxford University Press, 1970).
28. Fraser, *Warrior Queens*, 119.

Further Reading

FRAZER, ANTONIA. *The Warrior Queens: The Legends and the Lives of the Women Who Have Led Their Nations in War*. New York: Random House Vintage, 1990. Good brief accounts of both women as well as some discussion of the concept of a warrior queen.

STONEMAN, RICHARD. *Palmyra and its Empire: Zenobia's Revolt Against Rome*. Ann Arbor, University of Michigan Press, 1992. One of the few books dealing solely with this subject.

TACITUS. *Annals of Imperial Rome*. London: Penguin Books, 1956. An excellent Roman primary source for the first century of the empire.

WEBSTER, GRAHAM. *Boudica. The British Revolt Against Rome AD 60*. London: Routledge, 1993 (revised edition). The best account of this revolt.

CHAPTER 8

Irene and Wu Zhao: Two Iconoclasts

What qualities do women rulers need in order to succeed in a society dominated by men? What criteria should be used by historians to evaluate their careers?

The word *iconoclast* has two different but related meanings. Originally, this word (literally, "image breaker") referred to Greek Christians in the Eastern Roman or Byzantine Empire who opposed the use of images in religious worship. A modern dictionary notes that an iconoclast is, more commonly, "one who attacks and seeks to overthrow traditional or popular ideas or institutions."[1]

Empress Irene, ruler of the Byzantine Empire for much of the period of 780–802 C.E., was most certainly not an iconoclast in the religious sense of the term; in fact, she was perhaps the most famous opponent of the eighth-century image breakers, and she helped ensure their defeat. However, both Irene and her near-contemporary, Chinese Empress Wu Zhao (625–705 C.E.), were iconoclasts in the more modern sense of that term. In the ancient world, women were not considered qualified to rule. Although royal women in ancient Egypt occasionally exercised power, the most famous of these, Hatchepsut (reigned 1486–1468 B.C.E.), chose to be portrayed as a "king" rather than a queen, since it was easier for a woman "to adapt herself to fit the titles than to change the titles to fit her sex."[2] When she died, her nephew tried to destroy all evidence that she had ruled. Both Wu Zhao and Irene attacked the widespread conviction that ruling a large state was a distinctly male task. Although both began by ruling in the names of their husbands or sons, each also eventually went beyond this to rule in her own name. Both also governed their states successfully enough that even some male critics admitted their competence. Both were also accused of much intrigue, and each saw such behind-the-scenes maneuvering as the only way to secure power in a man's world.

Facts about the early years of Irene are scanty. Born in Athens and orphaned early in life, her piety and dazzling beauty brought her to the attention of Emperor Leo IV, who married the seventeen-year-old in 769. Beginning with eighteenth-century English historian Edward Gibbon, who referred to Irene's "haughty spirit" and to her ambition which "stifled every sentiment of humanity and nature," historians have gone out of their way to condemn Irene's character.[3] Words such as *unscrupulous, cruel,* and *diabolical* are used to describe her actions and intentions. Of her desire for power, there is little doubt; whether her use of that power was wise or not is open to interpretation.

Even had she sought power in a more traditionally feminine fashion and exercised it behind the scenes, Irene would be famous for her role in the iconoclast controversy. Her husband, a determined opponent of images, enforced a church council decree of 754 that made anyone who possessed or used "the evil art of painters" in worship an enemy of both church and state. Supported by the army, court clergy, and upper classes, who saw the use of images as idolatry, the emperor forced the masses to take an oath swearing they would not worship images. Most monks supported the use of paintings as proper devotion and, because of this, many monasteries were seized by the state during the mid-eighth century and turned into barracks and arsenals for the army. Women were particularly suspected of being iconophiles ("lovers of images"), and Irene herself was accused of being "lying and unscrupulous" because she presumably hid her iconophile views until the death of Leo IV in 780.

For the next ten years, Irene ruled the Byzantine Empire as regent for Constantine VI, her ten-year-old son. During this time, she made peace with the Muslim Arabs in 783 and sought a closer relationship in the West with Emperor Charlemagne and the Roman papacy. Her most notable achievement, however, was to secure a decree from a church council in 787 which officially restored the use of images in churches, noting (as did the Western Roman Church) that such pictures of Christ and the saints were to be "venerated" and not "adored." The monks or "devout party" were victorious and they hailed Irene as "the Christ-supporting Empress, whose government . . . is a symbol of peace."[4]

Such praise from the monks did little to endear the empress to the iconoclastic military men who blamed her for their military defeats at the hands of the Bulgars (788) and Muslims. Irene also withheld all power from her son and gave it to her favorites, especially the eunuch [castrated] Stauracius. Army opposition to Irene led to mutiny in 790, and Irene was forced to turn over the government to her son Constantine VI. This is when the real intrigue began.

Irene spent the next two years rebuilding her "power base." According to Edward Gibbon, Irene "flattered the bishops and eunuchs, revived the filial tenderness of the prince, regained his confidence, and betrayed his credulity."[5] By 792, Irene, who was once again called the empress, was an unofficial co-ruler with Constantine. She would not be content until she secured full control of the state. Though critics accused her of plotting to bring about Constantine VI's downfall, this was not hard, since Constantine assisted in weakening himself. In 792, when his uncles threatened the throne, he punished them by blinding the eldest and cutting out the tongues of the other four. Irene's critics say she "persuaded" him to do this. While she may or may not have been behind this maiming, it is certain that she encouraged Constantine's fondness for and adultery with one of her servant girls, Theodote, whom he married after divorcing his wife. When the devout monks protested this relationship, he lost patience and finally arrested, beat, and imprisoned a group of them at the Sakkudion monastery. Whatever Irene's role in all this, Constantine's behavior does not mark him as an effective ruler.

Little love was lost between mother and son during their seven years of joint rule. By the summer of 797, Irene was actively conspiring against her son. Once he became aware of this, Constantine fled the capital city of Constantinople but was soon arrested on the Asiatic shore of the Bosphorus. At Irene's orders, the punishment he had inflicted upon his eldest uncle was visited upon Constantine: His eyes were put out so that he could never rule again. This was the heinous crime that Gibbon believes "may not be paralleled in the history of crimes."[6] In Irene's defense, we should note that her behavior was little different from that of earlier, male rulers. Besides, she could have killed Constantine outright. But that would have been murder—and much more sinful.

Despite the reproach historians heaped upon Irene, the last five years of her reign were prosperous and peaceful for her and the empire. She patronized the arts, built convents, and contributed considerable sums to charity. More important, by lowering taxes and import duties, she provided genuine help to her poor subjects, who had been abused by tax collectors. And, as Irene rode to church in a golden chariot pulled by four white horses, she scattered money among the poor who lined the streets.

Unfortunately, Irene's victory did not bring an end to either the iconoclast controversy or plots by the palace nobility and eunuchs. A combination of lingering religious resentments and palace intrigue led to her overthrow in 802. After her former finance minister Nicephorus seized the throne, she made a dignified speech and then spent her last year of life in exile, supporting herself by spinning on the island of Lesbos. She might have been comforted had she known that the iconoclasts, in the end, would lose their fight to ban images. When that day came, the clergy whom she had consistently supported saw to it that this proud, passionate, and ambitious woman was made a saint of the Greek Orthodox Church. She became "the most pious Irene."

Irene of Byzantium appears saintly when compared with Wu Zhao, the woman who moved from concubine to sole ruler of Asia's most powerful empire. Wu Zhao's Chinese Empire was larger than that of Irene, her tenure of power longer, and her sins of greater enormity; for her, murders and plots were almost routine. Wu Zhao, like Irene, seized and held power by intrigue.

Born in 625, Wu Zhao was thirteen when she became a Concubine of the Fifth Grade at the court of Emperor Taizong in 638. Her beauty and ambition gave her an advantage over the 122 concubines of various "grades" at the Tang emperor's court in Changan. Although imperial concubines were supposed to be strictly secluded from all but the emperor, Wu Zhao fell in love with the emperor's son and slept with him before Taizong died in 649. Her morally reprehensible but practical liaison with the future emperor is an example of Wu Zhao's shrewdness; it alerts us to a talent she exploited throughout her career.

Following Taizong's death, his wives and concubines were sent, as was customary, to a Buddhist convent where they were expected to live out their days quietly. Within eighteen months, however, Wu Zhao was back at the palace as a concubine of her old lover, the new Gaozong emperor. Empress Wang encouraged her husband to resume his old relationships in the hope that Wu Zhao would displace another concubine who had borne Gaozong a son, as the empress had not. Her plan backfired tragically. Wu Zhao gave the emperor a son in 653 and maneuvered skillfully against both her rivals; she even accused the empress of the murder of Wu Zhao's second child.

From 654 to 655, court officials opposed efforts by Wu Zhao and the emperor to depose Empress Wang so that Wu Zhao could have her position. It was not until November 655 that a key official served to legitimize their undertaking by writing that it was a family matter and not an affair of state. Immediately, the empress and the former favorite concubine were accused of trying to poison the emperor, "degraded," and thrown into prison. When the emperor treated the two women kindly even after they were imprisoned, Wu Zhao was infuriated and sent executioners to beat "the two unfortunate women with a hundred blows, cut off their feet and hands, and then throw them, bound, into a brewing vat." When they died several days later, their bodies were decapitated and cut to pieces.[7]

It is reported that Wu Zhao had nightmares about this incident and in later years preferred to spend most of her time at Loyang, the "eastern capital," in order to avoid being reminded of her early misdeeds in Changan. As empress she was soon able to console herself with power. Her son Li Hong was appointed crown prince in early 656 and, within three years, all the elder statesmen of the Tang dynasty who had opposed her appointment had been degraded.

When Gaozong suffered a stroke in 660, Wu Zhao conducted the business of state for the next two years. She sat behind him, hidden from petitioners by a screen, and advised him during formal audiences. Even when healthy, Gaozong had not been a strong ruler; he had apparently let the empress handle many affairs of state because it was easier for him, she was competent, and she used sex to control him. One of the official histories described the situation that existed until Gaozong's death in 683: "The whole sovereign power of the empire passed into her hands; life or death, reward or punishment, were decided by her word. The Son of Heaven sat on his Throne with folded hands, and that was all. Court and country called them the Two Holy Ones."[8]

One of the most interesting features of Empress Wu Zhao's personality was her strong sense of purpose and individuality. In sharp contrast with Irene, who consistently served the "devout party" in Byzantium, Wu Zhao depended on no one—she served no party, court faction, or family. This self-serving attitude is clear from her treatment of her own family. When her half-brother chided her for advancing her mother and blood relatives at court, she decided to teach him a lesson. She told the emperor that it would look better if some of her relatives were transferred to distant posts—and off went her half-brother. Sometime later, she killed two birds with one stone by apparently poisoning her niece, who had caught Gaozong's eye, and then blaming the death on her two troublesome nephews, who were then executed.[9] Her behavior contrasted dramatically with that normally expected in a society in which attachment to family was one of life's most important virtues. She did not want to become the pawn of her family, the usual fate of empresses. Her victory resulted in widespread condemnation, much of it deserved, most of it written after her death.

During her lifetime, which encompassed the reigns of her husband and two of her sons, as well as the period from 690 to 705, when she ruled in her own name, Wu Zhao's critics were muted by her ruthless use of power and personal ability. During Gaozong's reign, she used her power over him to arrange the downfall of real or potential opponents. After his death, she ruled through her sons and with the aid of an efficient secret police force, which she disbanded once she took sole power.

Wu Zhao was an effective ruler. To call her decisive is perhaps an understatement, given what we have seen of her style of rule. Yet she combined decisiveness with an intelligent grasp of political problems and the wisdom to employ able administrators who owed their position and power entirely to her. The Chinese Empire was peaceful and powerful throughout most of Wu Zhao's reign. She patronized literature and art and was especially supportive of Buddhism. She established state hospitals and supported scholars at court. Wu Zhao also established a reward and promotion system for state officials and cut back on expenses for public works in order to save money. In the 670s, the empress decreased military expenses but only after she had played an important role in the conquest of Korea in the previous decade. Like her Byzantine counterpart, Wu Zhao lowered taxes for the poor. By the time of his death, Gaozong had so much confidence in Wu that he asked in his will that his successor defer to her "in all matters pertaining to military and civil affairs."[10]

Wu Zhao and Irene not only shared a concern for reducing taxes on the lower class but also enjoyed at least one other common trait. After holding power in the name of weak male rulers, each decided to rule in her own name. Wu Zhao went even further by deciding to establish a new dynasty, a major change in the Chinese political system. Both women showed considerable patience. It took several years for Irene to arrange the ouster of the son who had severely weakened himself. It took six years, from 684 to 690, for Wu Zhao to plan and execute a change of dynasty. Both women had to find ways to make their power seem legitimate. Irene did this by supporting the "devout party," which favored the use of images. Wu Zhao also used religion. Since imperial power was sacred, Wu Zhao could not simply claim to be "the best person for the job." Heaven—with some aid from her officials—had to approve so serious a change. In 688, a stone found in the Luo River was said to contain a "mystic inscription" which proclaimed "the Holy Mother has come among men to rule with perpetual prosperity." This clear omen of the need for a change was honored with an elaborate ceremony in which the Luo River was deemed sacred. (While this gave the river no healing qualities, it made fishing in it a sacrilege.) Several years later, after several formal requests from her officials, Wu announced the end of the Tang dynasty; all members of her own family were given princely rank and her ancestors were posthumously deified. [After her death, however, the Tang dynasty was restored.]

Wu Zhao ruled alone three times longer than Irene—a full fifteen years—despite revolts and intrigues against her. The change of dynasty name made her even more wary of family members who wanted to take power. She wanted power for herself; she was not very concerned about the future of her family, or her reputation. Her actions outraged the Confucian scholars, and the bureaucrats bewailed the rule of a woman, especially one who behaved as she did. She caused scandal, for instance, by adopting young men as her favorites at court. Yet the soldiers obeyed orders, the peasants tilled their fields, and people were generally content. It is tempting to suggest that by ruling as successfully as they did, Empresses Wu Zhao and Irene might serve as role models for today's feminists. At least for a short time, these women challenged the convention that women should not rule. Are they then the spiritual ancestors of the female political leaders of today? The answer must be a qualified no.

Neither Irene nor Wu Zhao saw themselves, based upon the evidence we have, as advocates for women. They clearly wished to secure power for themselves for the same reasons which motivated men. It is interesting that neither the Byzantines nor the Chinese had a term equivalent to our term *empress*, which we use to designate a sole woman ruler. Irene signed her decrees as *basilius*, the masculine term for ruler; Wu Zhao was known as "Holy and Divine Emperor," since there was no word in Chinese to indicate a female ruler. Both of these women, like Egyptian Queen Hatchepsut nearly 2,000 years earlier, were content to use male titles—as long as they carried the titles and had the power.

This does not mean, however, that these women were not as iconoclastic as some of today's feminists. In the Greek Orthodox tradition, women were to be saintly and, in the Chinese tradition, they were to be submissive. The careers of Irene and Wu Zhao show that these stereotypes do not always reflect reality—that, like men, women rulers are capable of crimes and wickedness. This, too, helps destroy a stereotype. Irene and Wu Zhao were courageous and capable politicians. In their patriarchal society, this was not enough for success. They had to be revolutionaries, for they had to reject the legal and moral restraints of their culture. In the words of Wu Zhao's biographer, C. P. Fitzgerald, women such as Wu Zhao were "true revolutionaries" because they had to "repudiate, in their hearts, all the mental barriers which men have built to restrain the use of open violence. The laws, the moralities and the conventions are to women the toys of men; to be played when no essential issue is at stake, but to be cast on one side without a second thought the moment that any really vital need arises."[11]

Fitzgerald's analysis may itself be marred by some traditional Western attitudes about women, most notably the image of women as immoral seductresses that goes back to Eve in the book of Genesis. Perhaps the immoral behavior and the crimes of Irene and Wu Zhao would have been passed over by the historians if these rulers had been male—or if the historians had been female. Fortunately or unfortunately, depending on your bias, neither was the case.

If Irene and Wu Zhao were not feminists in the precise modern sense of that term, they were successful female rulers. All modern historians admit Irene's role in preserving the use of images in Greek Christianity. Wu Zhao did more to preserve Tang power than to destroy it, despite her temporary change of dynasty. Her grandson, Xuanzong, became the most famous Tang ruler, and the Tang period is generally admitted to be the most brilliant in Chinese cultural history. These women were not feminists; they were rulers whose successes compare well with those of twentieth-century leaders such as Golda Meir, Margaret Thatcher, and Indira Gandhi. Perhaps if more people knew of the achievements of Irene and Wu Zhao, fewer would be surprised by the rise to power of these modern female political leaders.

Notes

1. *The American Heritage Dictionary of the English Language,* 3d ed. (New York: Houghton Mifflin, 1992), 894.
2. Vern L. Bullough, *The Subordinate Sex: A History of Attitudes toward Women* (New York: Penguin Books, 1974), 34–45. See Joyce Tyldesley, *Hatchepsut: The Female Pharaoh* (London: Viking, 1996), 129–136.
3. Edward Gibbon, *The Decline and Fall of the Roman Empire,* vol. IV (Philadelphia: John C. Winston, 1845), 197. The most hostile of the recent historians is Charles Diehl, author of *Byzantine Empresses,* translated from the French by Harold Bell and Theresa de Kerpely (New York: Knopf, 1963), chapter IV on Irene, 65–93. Diehl is also author of the pertinent section of vol. IV of the *Cambridge Medieval History* (New York: Macmillan, 1923), "Leo III and the Isaurian Dynasty," 1–26.
4. *The Cambridge Medieval History,* vol. IV, *The Eastern Roman Empire* (New York: Macmillan, 1923), 21.
5. Gibbon, *Decline and Fall,* IV, 197.
6. Ibid., 198.
7. C. P. Fitzgerald, *The Empress Wu,* 2d ed. (London: Cresset Press, 1968), 31; to degrade was, literally, to move someone from a higher to a lower grade in the official hierarchy. Often officials who were degraded were sent to the provinces; sometimes they were "accidentally" killed on the way. Our version of degrading, known as demotion, is less severe.
8. From the *T'ung Chien Chi Shih Pen Mo,* quoted in Fitzgerald, *Empress Wu,* 47.
9. Fitzgerald, *Empress Wu,* 49.
10. Nora C. Buckley, "Wu Chao: Woman-Emperor of China," *History Today,* vol. 19 (September 1974): 620. (This spelling of Wu Zhao's name reflects the older, Wade-Giles system of transliterating Chinese names into English.)
11. Fitzgerald, *Empress Wu,* 109.

Further Reading

BUCKLEY, NORA C. "Wu Chao: Woman-Emperor of China," *History Today,* vol. 19 (September 1974): 614–624. Fun to read.

DIEHL, CHARLES. *Byzantine Empresses.* Translated from the French by Harold Bell and Theresa de Kerpely. New York: Knopf, 1963. See chapter IV for his dislike of Irene.

FITZGERALD, C. P. *The Empress Wu.* 2nd ed. London: Cresset Press, 1968. Best biography in English; uses Chinese sources extensively.

CHAPTER 9

Al-Ghazali and Aquinas: Faith and Reason

What is the proper balance between faith and reason in seeking to understand the Divine? How do two important Christian and Muslim thinkers differ on this question?

How can men and women know God or the Divine? Most major religions have sacred books or scriptures. Can we find God by studying these and having faith in their teaching? What about prayer or other forms of personal communication with God? Are such private, meditative, or intuitive approaches to the Divine adequate to secure salvation? And what about the use of reason, a very different approach: can we think our way to God, using either abstract reason or information secured through our five senses?

These questions are not easy. They have been asked and answered in different ways by scholars and religious thinkers worldwide. A thousand years ago, two intellectuals, one Muslim and the other Christian, became famous for their attempts to answer these questions. Abu-Hamid Muhammed al-Ghazali (1058–1111) and Thomas Aquinas (1225–1274) were both men of faith, convinced that God wanted them to study Him, but also to pray to Him. These men were theologians [the term means student of the Divine]. More importantly, Al-Ghazali and Aquinas both believed that reason should be used to support Divine revelation, yet differed in the extent to which they were willing to trust reason. Their works are still studied by their co-religionists. To be read—not just remembered—after seven or eight hundred years is a tribute of the highest sort for any writer or thinker

"One of the greatest Muslims after Muhammed," in the words of a modern biographer, Al-Ghazali was born in 1058 in the city of Tus, in the northeastern part of what is today Iran.[1] Al-Ghazali's father was a wool-spinner who died before his two sons came of age. He left money with a friend so that Abu-Hamid and Ahmad could acquire more than the elementary learning he had received. At age eleven, Abu-Hamid began his lifetime of study with visits to his local mosque or house of worship in Tus. In 1073 he traveled to a mosque at Gurgan 250 miles away for a year of further study. An encounter with robbers when Al-Ghazali's caravan was returning to Tus illustrates the boy's early commitment to learning. When the leader of the robbers took his notes, Al-Ghazali pleaded for their return. The robber returned them but laughingly asked what kind of knowledge this was if stealing notebooks could cause the young man to lose it. From that day forward Al-Ghazali resolved to commit his learning to memory.

Between 1077 and 1084, Al-Ghazali studied at Nishapur with the famous teacher Al-Juwayni. His curriculum included theology, philosophy, logic, and natural science, and it is reported that he soon began to overshadow his teacher. From Nishapur, Al-Ghazali was invited to join the scholars at the Seljuk court in Baghdad where Nizam-al-Mulk, the Sultan's chief minister, supported education and established theological colleges. When Al-Ghazali was named professor of theology at the college of Nizamiyah in Baghdad in 1091, he had reached the peak of the Islamic world of learning. Here the very popular teacher wrote several important works over a four-year period and had up to 300 students in attendance at some of his lectures. Yet, by the middle of 1095, he had become spiritually and intellectually dissatisfied with the learning he had acquired.

Perhaps one reason for his growing concern lay in the nature of Islamic theology. The word of God [Allah in Arabic] had been given to Muhammad (570–632 C.E.) as the Messenger of God and the founder of the Arab Islamic community. Since Muhammed was both the religious and political leader of this community and since the revelations of God to Muhammad in the *Qu'ran* were the source of all truth, both government and education were supposed to reflect Divine truth. A class of scholars in early Islam known as *ulema* [not priests] developed a body of law [the Shari'a] and a set of Traditions [*hadith*]; these latter were "sayings" about practical matters that were not treated explicitly in the *Qu'ran*. Using a somewhat complicated formula, each "saying" was traced back or "proven" to have come from the lips of Muhammad or one of his early followers. For a good

Muslim, all social, political, and economic behavior had to be sanctioned or justified by God's word as revealed through his prophet Muhammad.

As a Muslim thinker, Al-Ghazali of course had to have a good understanding of the *Qu'ran*, the Traditions, and the Shari'a. But by his day, there was another complication. When the Arabs conquered the Greek-speaking people of the eastern Mediterranean in the eighth century, they were confronted with the Greek philosophy that had heavily influenced the Christian world in earlier centuries. Some early Muslim rulers encouraged this "foreign science" of the Greeks because they found Greek thought helpful in medicine, astronomy, and mathematics. But other Greek ideas followed, among them the fundamental notion found in the works of Plato (427–347 B.C.E) and Aristotle (384–322 B.C.E.), that human reason can help men discover the Absolute or God. By 900 C.E., such ideas were being studied in Baghdad, the capital of the Abbasid Caliphate. Chief among the early Islamic philosophers were Avicenna (d. 1037). During his years as a professor at the Baghdad Nizamiyah, Al-Ghazali became painfully aware of the growing tension between theology based upon the *Qu'ran* and the work of the "foreign" thinkers. Some theologians even saw all theologians and philosophers as natural enemies because the first found truth in the revealed word of God and the other found it in reason.[2]

Al-Ghazali was among a group of thinkers known as Ash'arites, named after Abu'l-Hasan al-Ash'ari (873–935), who believed that human reason could be useful—but only in a very limited way—in support of Divine revelation. While at Baghdad, Al-Ghazali wrote two major works. The first, *Magasid al-Falasifah (The Aims of Philosophers)*, discussed major Greek ideas of logic, metaphysics, and natural science, as he understood these from the works of earlier thinkers. Many features of Greek thought pleased him and he particularly liked the Greek use of the syllogism, a logical device both he and Aquinas used widely in their writings.[3] Al-Ghazzali's second work, however, was titled *Tahafut al-Falasifah (The Incoherence of Philosophers)*. It warned the thoughtful Muslim that philosophic rationalism could not prove all that it claimed. In particular, Al-Ghazali asserted, there were three propositions of the philosophers that had to be condemned as beliefs "in violent opposition to Islam." These were: (1) the belief that the world is eternal, (2) "the assertion that Divine knowledge does not encompass individual objects" (i.e., that God sticks to the big picture and ignores little things like eclipses of the sun), and, (3) the philosophers' denial of the doctrine of the resurrection of bodies.[4]

Al-Ghazali initially wished to reconcile philosophy and theology to preserve the best insights of each for use by the other. During his early years in Baghdad, Al-Ghazali lived with the tension between these two ways of seeking truth, although he gave first place to theology. The strain that his position caused him finally began to take its toll. Since he found himself so often disagreeing with the religious scholar-jurists and trying to mediate disputes between them and the philosophers, Al-Ghazali began to wonder if either group was right. He became skeptical of ever discovering truth and he wondered at one point if perhaps people became Christians, Jews, or Muslims simply because of the way they were raised. By the summer of 1095, Al-Ghazali suffered from a speech impediment, perhaps caused by anxiety, and soon he could not eat. His doctors could not cure what they called his disease of the heart. Al-Ghazali resigned his prestigious position in the Abbasid capital. Later, he said he believed that his illness and departure from Baghdad were God's way of reclaiming him. His confusion, he wrote, was soon ended by "a light which God most high cast into my breast."[5] Al-Ghazali became a mystic.

Wherever they are found—and all religions have some— mystics tend to reject reasoning as a path to God. Islamic mystics, known as Sufis from the simple garment of suf or wool that the early ones wore, searched for God within the human soul. Like their Hindu, Christian, or Jewish counterparts, they relied on intuition or an "inner light" to acquire knowledge of God. Many mystics seek direct, personal contact with God through intense meditation, isolation from others, and strict disciplining of the body. Some seek absorption into the Divine [the goal of many Hindus] or even claim to identify themselves with God. This last claim, usually considered blasphemy or heresy by other believers, was not his view, and is at best "very difficult to explain," in Al-Ghazali's words.[6] For at least six years, Al-Ghazali lived as a mystic. His wanderings during these years included a stay in Damascus and a pilgrimage to Mecca and Medina, the two holiest cities in Islam. What he gained from these years of travel, prayer, and study was a new appreciation of personal, emotional religion. He wrote that Sufis "are the true travelers on the path of God, their behavior is the finest of all behaviors, their path is the rightest of all paths, and their character is the noblest of all characters."[7] Sufis tried to love God for God's sake, not out of fear of Hell, hope for Heaven, or because it was a reasonable thing to do. This made their faith pure. Because of his intellectual reputation, Al-Ghazali's Sufi beliefs helped guarantee Sufi thought a permanent and respectable place in the future of Islam.

Yet Al-Ghazali himself did not remain solely a Sufi mystic. After four years of traveling and meditating in mosques, he returned to Tus in 1099, probably to visit his family. According to biographers he had a wife, two daughters, and perhaps a son and had provided for their support and education before leaving Baghdad in 1095. In July 1106, Al-Ghazali returned to teaching at Nishapur, the provincial capital where he had first gone as a student nearly twenty years earlier. There he continued to work on his greatest work, *Ihya' 'Ulum al-Din (The Revival of the Religious Sciences)*, which he had begun during his Sufi wanderings. Finished only days before his death in 1111, the *Ihya'* became a classic work on how to become a good Muslim.

A large work, the *Ihya' 'Ulum al-Din* has four parts, each divided into ten books. The first part discusses the basic dogmas of Islam and the Muslim approach to knowledge. The second deals with the laws and everyday prayers and customs of Islamic life. In the third and fourth, Al-Ghazali reviews and studies the vices and virtues—lust, anger, greed, and vanity on the one hand, and love, fear, sincerity, self-discipline, and meditation on the other. *Ihya' 'Ulum al-Din* was a guide to the religious life. It did not ignore the philosophic insights that Al-Ghazali had once studied so carefully, but it certainly gave them second place. At one point he listed three levels of spiritual development. The lowest was having faith in the authority of others, the second was gaining knowledge of God through study or reasoning. The third and highest was personal insight or the "immediate experience" or "taste" of God spoken of by the Sufis.[8]

Despite his new conviction that personal, mystical experience was the best way to know God, Al-Ghazali remained an orthodox Muslim, obedient to the laws and respectful of the *Qu'ran* and traditions. He also remained committed to learning, as his return to teaching indicates. A medieval Christian would have called the "inner knowledge" that brings men to God "grace." Perhaps that is the way the views of Al-Ghazali were presented when they were translated into Latin and studied at the University of Naples, where the young Thomas Aquinas encountered them as a student in 1239–1244. Connections are difficult to trace in the history of thought, but it is interesting that Aquinas, who did study "Algazel" at Naples, agreed with his Muslim predecessor that contemplation of God [Truth] was distinctive to man and our highest goal.[9]

Thomas Aquinas was born in 1225 in the town of Roccasecca in southern Italy. His pursuit of God and Truth was no less intense than that of Al-Ghazali, but it was different, as his own personal situation was different and as the intellectual currents of his day differed from those of eleventh-century Baghdad. Thomas was the son of Count Landulf of Aquino, who wanted him to advance the family's power by becoming a Benedictine monk and head of the prestigious abbey of Monte Casino, where Thomas was sent to study as a child.

While a student at the University of Naples in 1244, Thomas decided to join the new Order of Preachers or Dominicans, a monastic group devoted to prayer, preaching, and study, but a group with much less prestige than that of the long-established Benedictine Order. Although his father had died the previous year, several of Thomas' brothers kidnapped him while he was on his way to Paris to join the Dominicans. They locked him in the family castle at Roccasecca and, according to one story, even tempted him with a prostitute to get him to change his mind for the sake of the family. He is said to have chased the prostitute from his room with a firebrand and continued his writing.[10] Thomas finally got to Paris and studied there for three years before traveling to Cologne to study with the famous theologian Albert the Great. Ordained a priest in 1250, Thomas received a degree as a Master of Theology six years later and began a life of teaching and writing in Paris, Naples, and Rome.

The intellectual challenge that Thomas Aquinas faced in thirteenth-century Europe was somewhat more complicated than that facing Al-Ghazali a century and a half earlier in Baghdad. Al-Ghazali's challenge was to establish a balance between mystical faith and one based upon the *Qu'ran*, tradition, laws, and philosophy. His solution was to restore or reaffirm the importance of personal, mystical "knowledge" in the life of a religious person.[11] For the Christian world of Aquinas' day, this was not a problem. Personal piety and mystical approaches to Divine Truth were perfectly acceptable, as were philosophical approaches. The challenge Aquinas and other orthodox thinkers faced was that some teachers, especially Siger of Brabant at the University of Paris, had separated faith and reason, giving undue importance to the latter, and were using the ideas of Aristotle, recently translated from Arabic, as their justification.

How did they do this? Prior to this time, of the two Greek "fathers" of Western philosophy, Plato and Aristotle, Plato proved more congenial to religious thinkers. Plato stressed what ought to be, the world of "forms and ideas" which he said existed "beyond" the material world. Thus, human love or patience was a mere "reflection" of the Ideal of perfect Love or perfect Patience that existed in the "realm of ideas" apart from this world. It was easy for early Christian thinkers to "baptize" Plato by simply assuming that the perfect "forms of ideas" he spoke of were really Divine Ideas that existed in Heaven or in the mind of God. Aristotle, once his work was rediscovered in the Latin West due to the early work of Muslim translators, proved more troublesome to Christian theologians. Aristotle stressed, not what ought to be, but what was. When dealing with the world of man and nature, Aristotle sought natural rather than supernatural explanations. Some things, he admitted, could never be proven. He argued, for example, that you cannot use reason to prove that the world is not eternal. With such admissions as these, Christian theologians could readily admit that many Christian tenets were impossible to prove by human reason. Men like Siger of Brabant took Aristotle literally and made little or no effort to supplement their study of his work with "the light of faith." Because of this, church officials first considered these men heretics and almost threw Aristotle's ideas (and those who taught them) out of all Latin Christian universities.

Thomas Aquinas joined battle against those who would turn either Aristotle or the Bible into idols, something to be worshipped without question or thought.[12] Wishing to affirm both Aristotle and traditional Christian faith, Thomas had to show how the views of Aristotle could complement rather that contradict Christian belief. Thomas argued, for example, that although natural things have natural causes, as Aristotle says, that fact itself does not deny the need for a Creator. There is no contradiction between "laws of nature" and a God who created those laws and allows them to operate (as the law of gravity does) automatically. When we do come upon an apparent contradiction such as Aristotle's belief that reason suggests the world is eternal, it is simply evidence, for Aquinas, that reason has its limitations; there are some truths that can only be understood with the eyes and ears of faith. Notice that on this very question of whether or not the world is eternal, Al-Ghazali said that the philosophers were simply wrong—they could not prove it.[13] Aquinas takes a different approach. He says they are right—as far as they go. The position that the world might be eternal is not unreasonable, but merely based upon incomplete evidence, a defect that only faith can remedy. Our faith, however, is strengthened if we will take the reason of Aristotle as far as we possibly can in discovering truths about ourselves, the world, and God. Reason is, after all, God-given. Thomas' attempt to combine or synthesize the thought of Aristotle with the faith of the Christian fathers and with scripture was generally successful.

Unlike Al-Ghazali, Aquinas wished to do more than give primacy to faith over reason; he wished to show that Aristotle and the church needed each other, could support and strengthen each other's case. This was a bold enterprise, this dual defense of Aristotle's philosophy against those who rejected it entirely as irreligious or heretical and against men like Siger of Brabant who agreed that it was irreligious but said "so what?" Although some of the ideas of Aquinas were confused with those of Siger and condemned by the church shortly after Thomas' death, the error was corrected and Thomas was named a saint by the church in 1322.

The great *Summa Theologica (The Sum of Theology)* contains much of the synthesis of faith and reason constructed by Aquinas. This massive work was begun in 1266 and left incomplete at his death in 1274. Often compared to a building because of the way the parts build upon each other, the *Summa* moves slowly and majestically from a discussion of God and his attributes and creations in part one through a discussion of "man's movement toward God" in parts two and three.[14] The structure takes a circular approach from God to man and back to God again and the argument is very tightly knit. Throughout, Thomas carefully distinguished "natural theology," or knowledge about God based upon human reason, from the truths given through revelation. Reason cannot help us understand angels but it can tell us much about human nature. In Thomas' *Summa*, all things follow one another logically; even the Christian doctrine of the Incarnation, which proclaims Jesus both

God and man and which was long considered a central mystery of faith, seems "logical" enough in the system of Aquinas. For many Roman Catholics the *Summa* of Thomas Aquinas continues to be just what the name implied.

Too much attention to the *Summa* can obscure Thomas the man. Described in one source as "tall, corpulent, and silent," there is a story that he had to have a crescent cut out of his desk to accommodate his stomach when he sat down.[15] When young he was reputedly called a "Dumb Ox" because he was very quiet in school. Aquinas, while slow to speak, apparently remembered everything he ever read or heard. While composing the *Summa*, he dictated 1,000 words a day, often using four secretaries at a time as copyists and remembering exact quotations in the process. He did this while performing the duties of a full-time university professor and devout priest. This life of intense study over a period of twenty years took its toll. On December 6, 1273, Thomas had "a mysterious experience, which some have interpreted as a vision and some as a mental breakdown." He stopped work on his *Summa* at that point and in three months was dead. After his experience on December 6, Thomas was said to have remarked to someone that he could no longer write "because all that I have written now seems like straw."[16]

It is tempting to compare Thomas' "mystical" illness with that of Al-Ghazali. Both seem to have been brought on by mental and physical exhaustion. Pious believers in both religions may see the illness of such intellectuals as a message from God urging them to return to the faith of the heart. In Al-Ghazali's case, that did happen; in the case of Aquinas, we are not sure. He did not live long enough for us to know whether he had a stroke, a conversion experience, or some combination of the two. What we can be sure of is that both Abu-Hamid Muhammad Al-Ghazali and Thomas Aquinas exemplified the role of the intellectual at his best in the Western world. Each man had a truth to profess, and did so courageously, risking his reputation. Each man remained true to the basic values of his religion and yet was open to new truth. Thus, both were able to expand the horizons of the intellectual and spiritual world in which they lived. Both were men of faith, but also willing—especially in the case of Aquinas—to consider the claims of reason. Even though Al-Ghazali was more suspicious of reason than Aquinas appeared to be, he was not as opposed to rational philosophy as some later Islamic thinkers would be. He "retained the right of reason to arbitrate in theological controversies," in the words of one scholar.[17]

However, the difference between Al-Ghazali's and Aquinas' attitudes toward the relative importance of faith and reason also reflects a difference between their two cultures. In Western Christian society at this time, in part due to the work of Muslim translators of Aristotle and of people like Siger and Thomas Aquinas, it was easier to study God using reason. Aquinas was neither the first nor the last Christian intellectual to try to prove the existence of God, for example, using reason. In Islamic society, in part due to the strong attacks on the philosophers who tried to interpret the words of the *Qu'ran* (such as reference to the "hands of God") metaphorically instead of literally, it soon became nearly impossible to utter anything but the most traditional and literal interpretation of the word of God—and survive.

Faith would remain—to this day—more important than philosophy in the Islamic world, while the use of reason would ultimately undermine religious faith for many people in Europe. The larger, longer view of this issue makes it clear that both Al-Ghazali and Aquinas, while influential among their contemporaries and co-religionists later, were also clearly products of the place and time in which they lived.

Notes

1. W. Montgomery Watt, *Muslim Intellectual: A Study of Al-Ghazzali* (Edinburgh: Edinburgh University Press, 1963), vii; the city of Tus no longer exists. It was destroyed in the fourteenth century by the conqueror Tamurlane, who literally cut off its water. [More recent scholars spell Al-Ghazali's name with one z.]

2. Philip K. Hitti, "Al-Ghazzali: Greatest Theologian of Islam," in *Makers of Arab History* (New York: Harper, 1971), 157.

3. The syllogism, e.g. "All men are mortal. John is a man. John is mortal" became a mainstay of medieval and much modern logic.

4. Al-Ghazali, *Tahafut al-Falasifah (The Incoherence of Philosophers)* translated by Sabih Ahmad Kamali (Lahore, Pakistan: Pakistan Philosophical Congress, 1958), 249; Majid Fakhry, *Islamic Philosophy, Theology, and Mysticism: A Short Introduction* (Oxford: Oneworld Publications, 1997), 71.

5. Watt, *Muslim Intellectual*, 47–66; W. Montgomery Watt, *The Faith and Practice of Al-Ghazzali* (London: George Allen and Unwin, 1953), 25; W. Montgomery Watt, *Islamic Philosophy and Theology: An Extended Survey* (Edinburgh: Edinburgh University Press, 1987), 86–88.
6. R. C. Zaehner, *Hindu and Muslim Mysticism* (New York: Schocken Books, 1969), 164; see A. J. Arberry, *Sufism: An Account of the Mystics of Islam* (New York: Harper & Row, 1970), 80, for Al-Ghazali's description of his conversion to Sufism.
7. Al-Ghazali, *Al-Munqidh*, quoted in Hitti, "Al-Ghazzali: Greatest Theologian," 164.
8. Watt, *Muslim Intellectual*, 151–164.
9. Hitti, "Al-Ghazzali: Greatest Theologian," 164.
10. James A. Weisheipl, *Friar Thomas d'Aquino: His Life, Thought and Work* (Garden City, New York: Doubleday, 1974), 29–35; Kenelm Foster, *Life of Thomas Aquinas* (Baltimore: Helicon Press, 1959), 129.
11. Majid Fakhry, *A History of Islamic Philosophy*. Second Edition (London: Longman's, 1983), 217–233, 247–251; Fakhry, *Islamic Philosophy, Theology, and Mysticism*, 70–71.
12. Josef Pieper, *Guide to Thomas Aquinas* (New York: New American Library, 1974), 115; see also the rest of this chapter.
13. Fakhry, *Islamic Philosophy, Theology, and Mysticism*, 71.
14. James Weisheipl, *Friar Thomas d'Aquino*, 220–221.
15. J. J. N. McGurk, "Thomas Aquinas, 1274–1974," *History Today* (April, 1974), 257; see also G. K. Chesterton, *Saint Thomas Aquinas* (New York: Sheed and Ward, 1933), 142–174.
16. Anthony Kenny, *Aquinas* (New York: Hill and Wang, 1980), 26; see Weisheipl, *Friar Thomas d'Aquino*, 322–23.
17. Fakhry, *Islamic Philosophy, Theology, and Mysticism*, 100; see also 101–104.

Further Reading

HITTI, PHILIP. *Makers of Arab History*. New York: Harper and Row, 1971. See pp. 145–166 for a good essay on Al-Ghazali.

McGURK, J. J. N. "Thomas Aquinas, 1274–1974," *History Today* (April, 1974), pp. 250–257. Describes Thomas the man and his contribution—briefly.

PIEPER, JOSEF. *Guide to Thomas Aquinas*. New York: New American Library, 1974. Short introduction to his philosophy for modern readers.

WATT, W. MONTGOMERY. *Muslim Intellectual: A Study of Al-Ghazzali*. Edinburgh: Edinburgh University Press, 1963. A good source but should be supplemented by Majid Fakhry, *A History of Islamic Philosophy*, Second Edition. London: Longman's, 1983.

CHAPTER 10

Marco Polo and Ibn Battuta: The Merchant and the Pilgrim

How did the predispositions of two famous medieval travelers color what they reported—and how they reported it? What was the most important difference and the most important similarity in the stories of these two travelers?

Today we can travel hundreds of miles by automobile or thousands of miles by air in a few hours. When we arrive at our destination, we can usually relax comfortably in a home or motel. Such was not the case seven centuries ago, when the English word *travel* originally meant the same as *travail,* that is, hard work that exhausted the body and tested the will.[1] Imagine how stressful it would be to live "out of a suitcase" for over twenty years and in the process risk serious illnesses and survive dangers posed by bandits, shipwrecks, pirates, trackless deserts, and frozen mountains.

These were only some of the problems faced by the two most famous world travelers in the pre-modern period. In 1271, Italian Marco Polo (1254–1324) set out with his father and uncle on a journey to the court of the Mongol Emperor of China, Kubilai Khan; he would not return to his native Venice until 1295. In 1325, a year after Polo's death, Islamic jurist Ibn Battuta (1304–1368) left his native city of Tangier in Morocco to begin a journey to the East that would take him a total of seventy-five thousand miles; he did not return home permanently until 1354.[2]

The thirteenth-century travels of Marco Polo and those of his fourteenth-century Muslim counterpart, Ibn Battuta, illustrate both the dangers travel posed in this period and the ways such dangers could be overcome. The Polo family was aided by the "Pax Mongolica," the period of peace established by Mongol rulers in the Asian steppelands from about 1250 to 1350. The strong control exercised by these rulers, in an empire which stretched from Persia to China, allowed the Polos safe passage to China and back. Fifty years later, when Ibn Battuta began his journey, the Pax Mongolica was more precarious, but hospitality and safety were provided to Muslims by a network of Muslim traders and rulers extending from Southeast Asia to the strait of Gibraltar.

Ibn Battuta traveled primarily in Muslim-ruled lands, the *Dar al-Islam* [House or Abode of Islam], while the Christian Polo, son of a European merchant, lived and worked in countries whose cultures and religions were foreign to him. This difference makes a comparison of their works most interesting. Marco Polo's knowledge of four Asian languages as well as Italian allowed him to communicate with foreigners and even work as an administrator for the Chinese emperor. Yet, in all his travels, he remained culturally an "outsider" to the peoples he met, and this fact enhanced his power of observation and stimulated his natural curiosity. By contrast, Ibn Battuta usually traveled as an "insider," and his hosts accepted him as a respected Muslim jurist *(qadi)* and student of Islamic mysticism (Sufism). Traveling to more than sixty Muslim courts, where he met rulers and their officials, Ibn Battuta was able to judge the behavior of his hosts in light of the Muslim scripture, the *Koran,* and the precepts of Islamic law. For him, the difference between their native cultures and his own North Arabic culture was of secondary importance.

We can be thankful that both men dictated accounts of their travels after they returned home—Polo, while in a Genoese prison in 1298, and Ibn Battuta, to a Moroccan scribe, Ibn Juzayy, 1354–1355. Since neither was trained to report objectively on the unusual customs of foreigners, both Polo and Ibn Battuta judged those they encountered by their own standards. Both travel accounts reveal the great diversity in Eurasian cultures during this period; both are laced with "miraculous" happenings and both amaze readers with fairly accurate accounts of the enormous wealth rulers had at their disposal. The chief difference between the two works is one of focus. Polo's *Travels* was written with a "merchant's eye for flourishing manufactures." It is marked, in the words of one biographer, with a "mercantile stamp."[3] Polo tells us little about himself but much about the social and economic practices of those he meets. He systematically discussed commerce, government, and customs with some attention to the spectacular and exotic. By contrast, Ibn Battuta focused on Islamic ritual practices and beliefs in the lands he visited. He was much more willing than was Polo to describe his own difficulties and good fortune and much less concerned with trade, commerce, and the forms of government. Ibn Battuta's *Rihla* (Arabic for *Travels*) described a personal journey, a pilgrimage. Indeed, Ibn Battuta began his journey intending to make only the pilgrimage to Mecca *(hadj)* required of all pious Muslims once in a lifetime.

Although Polo infused his *Travels* with a "mercantile spirit," he left Palestine in 1271 with a religious purpose. On an earlier journey to China, Marco's father, Nicolo, and his uncle Maffeo had been asked by the Great Khan (Kubilai) to bring back to the Mongol court some holy oil from Jerusalem and "a hundred men of learning, thoroughly acquainted with the principles of the Christian religion," who could make a case for Christianity. Kubilai Khan may have wished to compare the "wonders" of Christian priests with those of the holy men of other religions; evidence suggests, however, that his mother was a Christian, and his requests could have reflected a genuine interest in learning more about her faith.[4] Western Christian leaders, for their part, hoped to convert the Mongols to Christianity and use them as allies against the "infidel" Muslim Turks, whose lands lay between Christian Europe and China. Although such hopes were unrealistic, Pope Gregory X supplied the Polos with two priests and some oil from Jerusalem's shrine of the Holy Sepulchre; the priests, fearing attack, abandoned the Polos after traveling only a few hundred miles.

Without the priests, but with the oil and valuable "safe conduct" passes earlier provided by the Khan, the Polos crossed Asia Minor and reached the Persian city of Tabriz in 1272. From there they headed south to Hormuz on the Persian Gulf to take a ship to Southeast Asia and China. However, when they discovered that the Arab ships were held together with rope yarn instead of nails, they decided to travel overland through central Asia (Afghanistan and Tibet).

In Baku, southwest of the Caspian Sea, Polo encountered his first natural wonder, petroleum, which was used "as an unguent for the cure of rashes in men and cattle . . . and [was] . . . also good for burning." On the road to Hormuz, he encountered—as did Ibn Battuta decades later—the simoon, or "drying wind," of the desert, which could not only suffocate men but also dry out their corpses so that their limbs would fall off when men tried to remove them for burial.[5] While traveling through the Pamir Mountains and the Gobi Desert, the Polo party encountered the hardships associated with travels in thinly populated lands. In eastern Afghanistan, Marco fell ill and took a full year to recover; this is one of the few times in the *Travels* that he mentions his personal misfortunes. After leaving the city of Balach, the Polos entered a country where the people had fled to the mountains to escape bandits. As a consequence, local provisions were scarce and travelers had to carry enough food with them for themselves and their cattle. In the Pamir Mountains, the Polos saw no birds and noticed that their fires gave less heat because they were 15,600 feet above sea level. The Gobi Desert seemed to the Polos a place of hallucinations, "the abode of many evil spirits which lure travelers to their destruction with the most extraordinary illusions."[6]

The Polos were relieved once they left the Gobi and entered the northern Chinese province of Tangut (Gansu). There the party safely spent over a year, and the Polos had ample time to observe provincial customs and the many religions of the people: some of them were Saracens [Muslim], some were Nestorian Christian, and some were "idolaters" [Buddhists]. For the first time, Polo came upon a new fibre (asbestos), which "when woven into cloth and thrown in the fire . . . does not burn." But what fascinated the young traveler most were the marriage and sexual customs of the Asians. He recorded that, in Pem in central Asia, a woman could take another husband if her first husband was absent from home twenty days. "On the same principle," he added, men "marry wherever they happen to reside." In places, Polo found men willing to offer wives and daughters to strangers passing through. They believed this practice was "agreeable to their deities" and would bring them wealth and good fortune. The women, he added knowingly, were "very handsome, very sensual."[7] Polo described most of these customs matter-of-factly. In one Southeast Asian land he later visited, he calmly reported that no young woman could be married until "she has first been tried by the king." If the king liked her, he kept her around for a time, then dismissed her with a sum of money that would allow her to make an "advantageous match" within her class. Polo also noted that the king had 326 children. However, Polo was personally offended by a custom he encountered in Kanzhou, China. There men took as many as thirty wives and often married close relatives, even mothers-in-law. Polo considered this "like the beasts of the field." He also described as "scandalous" the Tibetan dislike of virgins; they expected unmarried girls to "have had previous relations with many of the opposite sex." This practice of judging a woman attractive on the basis of "the number of lovers she had" was due, he believed, to Tibetan paganism.[8] Polo did appreciate the strict marriage customs of the Mongols, which contrasted sharply with those of other Asians. Mongol women "excelled in chastity and decency of conduct," he wrote, and husbands remained loyal to their wives, though they could have as many of them as they could afford.[9]

Although some doubt Marco Polo's claims to have worked for Kubilai Khan for seventeen years,[10] he certainly displayed the characteristics of an accomplished courtier in his praise of Kubilai Khan as a "man of proved integrity, great wisdom, commanding eloquence, and celebrated valor," who was so virtuous that "wherever he went he found people disposed to submit to him."[11] Although his description of the Khan's court and its activities may have been exaggerated, Polo's account of the history, military organization, and social customs of the Mongols was accurate. Polo's European readers would later have trouble believing that Kubilai Khan kept a stud farm of ten thousand horses and mares, all "white as snow." They were also skeptical of Polo's claim that the Khan hunted with ten thousand falconers and hosted a state dinner so large that forty thousand people had to eat outside the hall. Yet, when one considers the size of the Mongol empire, of which China was only a part, Polo's estimates might be only slightly exaggerated. It is quite possible, despite the ridicule of Venetians, who referred to Marco as "il Milione," the man who speaks in millions, that Kubilai Khan's postal system (something like the American pony express) used two hundred thousand horses to supply ten thousand stations across Asia. It is also quite possible that the city of Hangzhou included 1,600,000 families and that some Tibetan monasteries housed up to 500 monks.[12]

Marco Polo claims that the Khan sent him on two long inspection tours, the first southwest through the modern provinces of Sichuan and Yunnan into Burma and the second southeast from Khanbalig, the site of modern Beijing, to the coastal cities of Kinsai and Zaiton (modern Hangzhou and Amoy). In describing these trips, as well as the journey home by sea through Southeast Asia and along the Indian coast, Polo's reporting followed a pattern. He opened with an account of the religion, government, and economic and commercial activity of the peoples he encountered. For example, he noted that, in the city of Nanjing, China, "the people are idolaters [Buddhists], use paper money . . . are subjects of the Great Khan, and are largely engaged in commerce. They have raw silk, and weave tissues of silver and gold. . . . The country produces a great deal of corn [grain]." Later, in discussing the island of Sumatra, Polo wrote:

> In this island there are eight kingdoms, each governed by its own king, and each with its own language. The people are idolaters [non-Christians]. It contains an abundance of riches and all sorts of spices, aloes wood, sapanwood for dyeing, and various other kinds of drugs, which, on account of the length of the voyage and the danger . . . are not imported into our country, but which find their way to the provinces of Manzi [South China] and Cathay [North China].[13]

Polo's account of conditions in Kinsai (Hangzhou) was particularly detailed. The city had a perimeter of a hundred miles, contained ten large marketplaces, and possessed paved roads that were guarded by watchmen on the lookout for fires. Polo was very impressed with both the well-organized government and the wealth of this trading center. On the door of his home, each head of household in Kinsai had to list the names of family members and the number of horses owned, so that authorities could keep constant track of city growth. The wealth of the city is suggested by the amount of pepper brought daily to the city; forty-three boatloads, each weighing 243 pounds, arrived daily. Kubilai Khan took in millions in revenue from this one city alone.[14]

Despite Marco Polo's focus on imports, exports, and local industry, he remained a child of his age—an age when people in every culture were fascinated with "miracles" and "wonders." One critic suggests that Polo preferred to write about the "popular culture" of everyday life rather than the "high culture" of Asia because he himself was culturally unsophisticated.[15] Polo never discussed art, philosophy, or literature, for example, but enjoyed mentioning such things as tattooing and cannibalism. While Polo did uncritically repeat stories of the miraculous, it is also true that most of his readers in fourteenth-century Europe believed them. They enjoyed reading about the one-eyed cobbler who saved the Christians in Baghdad from certain death by accepting a challenge from the Muslim caliph, praying, and moving a mountain. Polo's Christian readers were edified by his story of how the Church of St. John the Baptist in Samarkand remained standing after Christians complied with the order of the Muslim ruler to remove a portion of a central supporting pillar. These miracle stories are more credible than other Polo tales based on sheer fantasy: the existence of two islands 500 miles south of India, one inhabited only by males, and another thirty miles away inhabited only by females, or of birds on Madagascar large enough to pick up elephants in their talons and drop them on rocks to kill them.[16]

It is interesting that both Polo and his Muslim counterpart, Ibn Battuta, noted some of the same marvels during their journeys. How must contemporaries have viewed stories of dog sleds in Siberia, the practice of sati in Hindu India [widows throwing themselves on their husbands' funeral fires], or the burning of strange black stones (coal) to heat houses?[17] These things must have seemed as strange to the people of the fourteenth-century as moving mountains by prayer does to us.

The Polo party left China in 1292, charged by the emperor with delivering a new wife to Arghun, Khan of Persia. Supplied with large ships and many servants, the Polos took twenty-one months to complete their journey because of a five-month delay on the island of Sumatra. During the trip, nearly 600 members of the party died from various unspecified causes, but Marco Polo, his father, and his uncle finally returned to Venice, where they ended their lives as ordinary merchants.[18]

Ibn Battuta's journey, begun thirty years later, took him to more places than the Polos had visited. After leaving his home in the Moroccan coastal town of Tangier in 1325, Ibn Battuta wandered through the Nile valley and Syria and arrived in Mecca in 1326 for the first of four pilgrimages to that Holy City. During the next year, he visited Persia [then a Mongol state] and Iraq but returned to Mecca to engage in further study and religious meditation. Between 1328 and 1332, Ibn Battuta sailed southward down the east African coast to Kilwa and then turned back to visit Turkey, the Crimea, southern Russia, and the city of Constantinople. In 1333, he was in India, where he spent a number of years as the *qadi*, or Muslim judge, of Delhi. This largely honorific post paid well but also required him to spend much of his own money. Soon Ibn Battuta had a dangerous falling-out with the sultan of Delhi which nearly cost him his life; he returned to favor in 1341, when he was asked by the sultan to head a delegation to the emperor of China. Because of further adventures along the Mallabar (southwest) coast of India and in the Maldive Islands and Ceylon (Sri Lanka), the ambassador did not arrive in China until 1345, where he spent most of his time in the south. Between 1346 and 1349, the Arab jurist returned via Mecca to Tunis in North Africa and, during the next five years, he crossed the Sahara to visit Mali, a black African Islamic state in the western Sudan. In 1354, he returned to Morocco, where he completed dictating his *Travels* by December 1355.[19]

Since Ibn Battuta was a pilgrim, the central theme of his narrative is the insistence that one must live a properly pious, Muslim life. He expected his fellow Muslims to be devout in attending prayer services, to keep their women modest, and to show hospitality to strangers.

In his travels, Ibn Battuta visited Islamic holy men (pious shaykhs) and their tombs. In Cairo, Ibn Battuta visited the "great cemetery of al-Qarafa . . . a place of particular sanctity" containing "the graves of innumerable scholars and pious believers." At Hebron he discovered the graves of Abraham, Isaac, and Jacob and their respective wives.[20] He noted with disapproval the bad grammar of a preacher at Basra near the Persian Gulf and with approval that the Khwarizmians of central Asia beat people who missed the Friday prayer service, as he did when serving as a *qadi* in the Maldive Islands. He also tried to get women to dress modestly, but they refused to do so except when they were in his court. During periods of crisis or while waiting to begin another leg of his journey Ibn Battuta spent hours, even days, reciting the *Koran*.[21]

Throughout the *Rihla*, Ibn Battuta carefully noted which rulers and officials respected his status as a pilgrim and extended hospitality to him. Indeed, without the generosity of his hosts, he could not have continued traveling. Sultan Abu Sa'id of Iraq gave him a robe, a horse, and other provisions when he found out that Ibn Battuta was going to Mecca. One of the ruler's wives in Qaysariya in Iraq gave Ibn Battuta's party a meal and then presented him with a horse, with saddle and bridle, and money. In western Turkey, he stayed with a sultan who "every night sent us food, fruit, sweetmeats, and candles, and gave me in addition a hundred pieces of gold [and] a complete set of garments. . . ." Sultan Abu'l-Muzaffar Hasan at Kilwa was also praised for "his gifts and generosity"; this leader devoted "the fifth part of the booty made on his expeditions to pious and charitable purposes, as is prescribed in the *Koran*, and I have seen him give the clothes off his back to a mendicant who asked for them."[22]

Except for the times when he had been robbed or shipwrecked, Ibn Battuta traveled in style. He customarily journeyed with slaves of both sexes, many of them gifts to him or to his companions. While in Afghanistan, Ibn Battuta reported that his party "had about 4000 horses" as well as some camels. When sent to China as ambassador of the sultan of Delhi, Ibn Battuta took gifts of 100 horses, 200 slaves and dancing girls, fifteen eunuchs [castrated males], twelve hundred pieces of cloth, gold, silver, and other assorted presents. When Ibn Battuta visited "Adam's Foot," a mountain in Ceylon [modern Sri Lanka] revered by Hindus, Buddhists, and Muslims, he received an escort of four Hindu yogis, three Brahman priests, ten guards, and fifteen men to carry provisions.[23]

Ibn Battuta shared his personality with his readers more readily than did Marco Polo, and his text suggests he was a reasonably complex person. A lover of religious truth, correct ritual, and dogma, Ibn Battuta was also "fond of pleasure and uxorious" [inclined to dote on someone]. A recent scholar notes his "well-timed unctuousness" [excessively pious, smooth, or oily manner] and suggests that he may have wanted rulers to treat him with great honor because, in fact, he felt insecure about his own level of learning and legal abilities. While serving as a *qadi* in Delhi, for example, he was untrained in the particular school of law practiced there and could not even speak the language.[24] If it is true that this world traveler was personally insecure, it is remarkable that he tells us as much about his personal life as he does. He did not hide the fact that he flattered rulers in return for their money and favors. Yet Ibn Battuta was not a cynical politician but, like Marco Polo, a genuinely curious person who loved travel for its own sake and who could be sincerely generous and open with people. On the two chief occasions when he got in trouble with rulers, at Delhi and in the Maldive Islands, he attempted to play a political role for which he was unsuited. It is not surprising that he retreated to the life of a hermit after his narrow escape in Delhi and that he reentered the sultan's service to head the embassy to China because of his "love of travel and sight-seeing."[25]

Like Marco Polo, Ibn Battuta loved to share his discoveries with the readers; he, too, saw oil in Iraq and pearl divers in the Indian Ocean. He described the way Arab ships were built in the Persian Gulf and contrasted them with Chinese ships on which he later traveled. The strangest thing he saw was a slave in Southeast Asia who gave a long, flattering speech before his ruler and then cut his own throat—as a way of showing his great love for the sultan. This demonstration of loyalty was rewarded, for his family was given a large pension.[26]

The different personalities of Polo and Ibn Battuta are reflected in quite different styles of reporting. For example, in his accounts of the city of Quilon on the west coast of India, Polo the merchant commented on the amount of dyewood and fruit, as well as on the palm wine that "makes one drunk faster than the wine from grapes." He also noted the inhabitants' nakedness, except for a loin-cloth, and the fact that they marry close relatives. Ibn Battuta, by contrast, told the reader little about the flora, fauna, or people of Quilon. We are told that he arrived there after missing a ship in Calicut and losing nearly all his possessions; the most memorable thing about Quilon for Ibn Battuta was the quarrelsome, drunken porter who took him there from Calicut.[27]

As this example illustrates, while there is more ego evident in the *Rihla* than in Polo's *Travels*, Ibn Battuta's book contains more detailed cultural information and more exciting stories. Nowhere in Polo's book, for example, can one find a story to rival Ibn Battuta's account of how he escaped near death from bandits as he was leaving Delhi on his mission to China. After being pursued by and outrunning ten horsemen, he was then captured by forty bowmen and taken to their camp, where several men were assigned to kill him. His assassins lost their nerve, however, and allowed him to escape after he gave one of them (literally) the shirt off his back. He then wandered the countryside for six days, at one point eluding a band of fifty armed Hindus by hiding in a cotton field all day, until a kindly Muslim found him, took him home, and sent word to the members of his party, who returned and picked him up.[28] This close brush with death is only one of a half dozen reported in the *Rihla;* whether caused by illness, pirates, treacherous guides, stormy seas, or crocodiles, they are all presented believably but dramatically in the narrative.[29]

Both the merchant and the pilgrim give us a clear appreciation of how travelers, whether Christian or Muslim, merchant or jurist, viewed the world in the later medieval period. For both men, the world was a truly marvelous and sometimes miraculous place, where fact and fantasy intermingled in a way we find incomprehensible today. Even though they are not always reliable witnesses and were not writing history as we understand that term, both world travelers are praised by modern scholars for the practical information they recorded. In his book *The Discoverers,* historian Daniel Boorstin says of Marco Polo's book: "Never before or since has a single book brought so much authentic new information, or so widened the vistas for a continent." Other authors mention that a well-thumbed and annotated copy of Polo's *Travels* was found in Christopher Columbus's private library; the book may have helped Columbus decide to sail west to reach Asia because it describes Japan as a good fifteen hundred miles east of China. That would have placed it about where the Americas are located—if we take into account the smaller globe that Columbus would have used. Ibn Battuta's *Rihla* gives us the only information we have on many Muslim states in this period, especially those in West Africa and along the west coast of India.[30] Yet, despite the practical value of these two travel works, we should remember that they were written to entertain and to edify. Although Polo's work excited Europeans on the eve of an era of discovery and exploration, and Ibn Battuta's work confirmed for Muslims the essential religious unity of the *Dar al-Islam,* each man wrote to please himself and to charm his readers. That, as much as the information they contain, is what makes these two travel narratives interesting reading today.

Notes

1. Daniel J. Boorstin, *The Discoverers* (New York: Random House, 1983), 125.
2. Ibn Battuta's full name was Abu 'Abdallah Muhammad ibn Abdallah ibn Muhammad ibn Ibrahim al-Lawati ibn Battuta. In Arabic, "ibn" means "son of" and Lawata was the name of his particular Berber tribe; see Ross E. Dunn, *The Adventures of Ibn Battuta: A Muslim Traveler of the 14th Century* (Berkeley: University of California Press, 1986), 19.

3. *The Travels of Marco Polo,* edited with an introduction by Milton Rugoff (New York: New American Library, 1961), xxv; Richard Humble, *Marco Polo* (New York: G. P. Putnam's Sons, 1975), 55.
4. *Travels of Marco Polo,* 39; Henry H. Hart, *Marco Polo: Venetian Adventurer* (Norman: University of Oklahoma Press, 1967), 38–39; Humble, *Marco Polo,* 37–38.
5. *Travels of Marco Polo,* 51, 69; see H. A. R. Gibb, trans., *Ibn Battuta: Travels in Asia and Africa, 1325–1354* (London: George Rutledge and Sons, 1929), 120.
6. *Travels of Marco Polo,* 77, 81, 83–84, 89; Humble, *Marco Polo,* 85, 94.
7. Ibid., 87, 93, 94–95, 177–178; the Nestorians were declared heretics in the fifth century in a dispute over the nature of Christ. They established churches throughout Asia at this time.
8. Ibid., 96–97, 175, 236.
9. Ibid., 103.
10. A modern China scholar in Britain, Frances Wood, argued in *Did Marco Polo Go to China?* (Boulder, CO: Westview Press, 1996) that Polo traveled only as far as Constantinople (Istanbul) and that his information came from other travelers. Wood says, for example, that Polo included no Chinese or Mongol place names in his book and did not mention things he should have seen, such as the Great Wall and tea drinking. Some of Wood's critics point out, however, that the Great Wall as we know it was not built until after Polo's death and note Polo's accurate description of Kubilai Khan's capital. See John Larner, *Marco Polo and the Discovery of the World* (New Haven: Yale University Press, 2001), 58–65.
11. Ibid., 99; for more on Marco Polo's loyalty to the Mongol dynasty, see Leonardo Olschki, *Marco Polo's Asia* (Berkeley: University of California Press, 1960), 316–317, 397–404.
12. Ibid., 115, 117, 148, 156, 220; Humble, *Marco Polo,* 124, 206.
13. *Travels of Marco Polo,* 202–203, 238.
14. Ibid., 209–221; Humble, *Marco Polo,* 160–164.
15. Leonardo Olschki, *Marco Polo's Asia,* 145.
16. *Travels of Marco Polo,* 57–59, 85–86, 268.
17. Ross Dunn, *Adventures of Ibn Battuta,* 314–316; Gibb, *Ibn Battuta's Travels,* 150, 191–192; *Travels of Marco Polo,* 161, 249.
18. *Travels of Marco Polo,* xxi–xxiii; Humble, *Marco Polo,* 191–206; Hart, *Marco Polo,* 159–160.
19. For a brief account of Ibn Battuta's itinerary, see pp. 2–8 of Gibb, *Ibn Battuta's Travels.* There is a dispute among scholars concerning just how much time Ibn Battuta spent in Mecca during his second visit. He claims he was there until 1330, but that would give him insufficient time to reach India by 1333 and visit all the places he said he visited

before arriving in India. The dates used in this essay are ones suggested, on the basis of evidence in the *Travels* themselves, by Ross E. Dunn; see his *Adventures of Ibn Battuta*, 106, and notes on pp. 132–133 and 181–182.

20. Gibb, *Ibn Battuta: Travels*, 51, 55.
21. Ibid., 87, 168, 239, 243–244, 250.
22. Ibid., 101–102, 112, 131, 134.
23. Ibid., 180, 214, 258; see also 152, 236, 246–247, and Dunn, *Adventures*, 165, 177 for other examples of gifts given to Ibn Battuta and for examples of his desire to travel in comfort.
24. Gibb, *Ibn Battuta: Travels*, 2; Dunn, *Adventures*, 149, 311–312.
25. Dunn, *Adventures*, 197–209, 238–239; Gibb, *Ibn Battuta: Travels*, 212–213; Lucile McDonald, *The Arab Marco Polo* (Nashville: Thomas Nelson, 1975), 122–135; see also Ivan Hrbek, "Ibn Battutah," *Encyclopedia Britannica*, vol. 9 (Chicago: Benton, 1974), 144–145.
26. McDonald, *Arab Marco Polo*, 37, 49; *Travels of Marco Polo*, 228–229, 247; Gibbs, *Ibn Battuta: Travels*, 121–122, 177, 235–236, 243, 268–269, 277–278.
27. *Travels of Marco Polo*, 259–260; Dunn, *Adventures*, 225.
28. Dunn, *Adventures*, 215–216; Gibb, *Ibn Battuta: Travels*, 215–222.
29. For some other close calls, see Dunn, *Adventures*, 129–130, 155, 243–247; Gibb, *Ibn Battuta: Travels*, 261–265.
30. Boorstin, *The Discoverers*, 138; *Travels of Marco Polo*, xi; Joseph and Frances Gies, *Merchants and Moneymen: The Commercial Revolution, 1000–1500* (New York: Thomas Crowell, 1972), 130; Dunn, *Adventures*, 5.

Further Reading

ABERCROMBIE, THOMAS. "Ibn Battuta: Prince of Travelers," *National Geographic* (December 1991): 2–49. Compares how the lands Ibn Battuta visited have changed (or not changed) in six centuries.

DUNN, ROSS E. *The Adventures of Ibn Battuta: A Muslim Traveler of the 14th Century.* Berkeley: University of California Press, 1986. Best account of both the man and his times.

LARNER, JOHN. *Marco Polo and the Discovery of the World.* New Haven: Yale University Press, 2001. Excellent account of Polo that includes a history of his book as well.

The Travels of Marco Polo, edited with an introduction by MILTON RUGOFF. New York: New American Library, 1961. Inexpensive and well-footnoted edition for general readers.

CHAPTER 11

Mansa Musa and Louis IX: Pilgrims and State-Builders

How did the institution of monarchy differ in Europe and West Africa in the thirteenth and fourteenth centuries? In a religious age, does a king show he is powerful by being pious or does his piety help him become powerful?

It must have been a memorable sight. Imagine ninety camels loaded with gold, and 500 slaves marching before the king, each slave carrying a gold staff weighing four pounds. Such was the scene that July day in 1324 when Mansa Musa [*Mansa* means "King" in the Mandingo language] of Mali, the most powerful West African state, emerged from the sands of the Sahara and entered Cairo, Egypt.

Mansa Musa (reigned 1307–1337) was a pilgrim, a Muslim making a *hadj,* or holy journey, to Mecca in Arabia (today Saudi Arabia), the birthplace of Muhammed.

Now imagine another occasion, three generations earlier, when a second foreign monarch is making his way toward that same Egyptian capital. King Louis IX of France (1214–1270) has just landed an army of European knights at the port of Damietta on the Egyptian coast. The sultan's troops have fled and the king has decided to march on Cairo. It is the summer of 1249, and he wishes to conquer Muslim Egypt as a prelude to "recapturing" the Christian holy places in Palestine.

King Louis IX was also a pilgrim, but the goal of his holy journey was a military one, one battle in a war in which people could gain grace and even Heaven by conquering land for their God and by converting or destroying the infidel.

Louis of France, "the most Christian king," never reached his goal. Disease and rash action by some of his knights who got themselves trapped in the city of Mansourah prevented the king from conquering Egypt for the faith. Louis was captured by the Saracens, as the French called their opponents; he ransomed himself by returning the city of Damietta, and he finally returned to France in 1254. Mansa Musa, on the other hand, spent several months (and much gold) in Cairo before continuing to Mecca. He returned home the following year, poorer but still a powerful and pious ruler. Both of these men were remembered long after their deaths because of their holy journeys. France and the Sudanese kingdom of Mali were very different in political structure and culture. Yet the Muslim and pagan world of Mansa Musa and the Christian kingdom of Louis IX shared one characteristic: in both, religion was powerful enough a political force that a ruler could gain, keep, and demonstrate power through religious actions.

When he left for Mecca in 1324, Mansa Musa ruled over a kingdom that covered most of western Sudan.[1] Mali extended west from the Adrar des Ifores to the Atlantic just north of the mouth of the Senegal River and included much of the coast from that river south to what is now Ghana. Mansa Musa's kingdom was the largest of the three West African states that flourished between 700 and 1600 C.E. Mali power was created primarily by Sundiata, Mansa Musa's great uncle, during the first half of the thirteenth century— at the same time Louis IX was consolidating his control over French barons prior to embarking on his first crusade. Within a century after Mansa Musa's death in 1337, the power of Mali would be eclipsed by that of its former tributary state, the Songhai Empire.

Gold taken from the Bure area along the upper reaches of the Niger River formed the basis of Mali wealth. For centuries, the people of the Sudan had traded gold and slaves with the Muslim North African states across the Sahara. Since the West Africans had long provided much of the precious metal that supported the commerce of the Muslim Mediterranean and western Asian countries, the gold that Mansa Musa took on his pilgrimage was notable only because of its quantity. Muslim merchants had long criss-crossed the Sahara with salt, iron, clothing, and spices, which they traded for the gold and slaves of Ghana and Mali.

The Arab and Berber nomads from the north also brought their religion with them to the West African bazaars. Islam was a religion of attractive simplicity, with no priests or elaborate ritual. The obligation to pray daily, fast one month a year, and make a journey to Mecca once in your lifetime were its central tenets. Perhaps more important in explaining why many West African rulers and traders turned to Islam were the essential skills that Muslims from the north brought with them: writing and reckoning. Muslims did not send out missionaries explicitly to convert unbelievers, as Christians did, and this may explain why Islam remained a "ruler cult" in Mali and other West African states. The majority of African peasants remained attached to their older nature religions. Only the upper classes in Mali were Muslim for personal and economic reasons, and they were not particularly troubled that the lower classes were not.[2] The Muslim traveling scholar, Ibn Battuta, visiting Mali in 1352–1353 during the reign of Mansa Musa's brother Sulayman, noted some of the "pagan" customs he observed at court. Petitioners humbled themselves before the king by covering themselves with dust; when the king commended one of his men, they sprinkled more dust on their heads and backs in appreciation. Ibn Battuta noticed that even the Islamic inhabitants of Mali often ate "animals not ritually slaughtered, and dogs and donkeys." Young women, "even the king's daughters," appeared naked in public.[3]

The un-Muslim behavior of persons at Mansa Musa's court is more understandable when we appreciate the nature of kingship in West African societies. Mali was not a territorial state of the modern sort; it was certainly not a nation, as we generally use that term. Mansa Musa's subjects were members of various status groups (noble, freeman, serf, slave) or occupational categories (hunter, fisherman, trader, farmer). These people were also members of various tribal or ethnic categories, such as Soninke and Malinke, which were themselves subdivided, often into groups of villages, each headed by a chief. The king of such an agglomeration of occupational, ethnic, and kinship groups was rather like the leader of a very large family, with each branch of the family, or clan, agreeing to provide the leader with tribute in the form of money, slaves, grain, and arms. Such allegiances were historically weaker and more temporary than they might have been if the king had been seen as the head of a fixed territory and, in some sense at least, the "owner" of the land, as was the case in France. Although West African kings, like European ones, had personal lands from which they drew an income, Mansa Musa had to hold his empire together by bonds of personal and family loyalty. This loyalty was based on how strong the "great man," or ruler, was and on what he could do for his various peoples. The collection of taxes, as well as military service to the ruler, often depended upon how strong the king was perceived to be, not on his territorial or legal rights.

This system of West African kingship helps explain why Mansa Musa (and some of his predecessors in Mali) relied on court ritual and went on elaborate pilgrimages to Mecca. It was a way of showing strength and confidence, for only a strong ruler could command such public obedience and be absent from his kingdom for over a year. This display of strength would consolidate his rule at home upon his return and win him prestige in the wider Islamic community. At least, that is what Mansa Musa hoped would happen, and it seemed to work for him. It is not accidental that, on his way back from Mecca, he stopped in Gao to "receive the submission" of the Songhai ruler, one of his strongest potential enemies.

There is no doubt that he had impressed his Muslim brethren in the north. The king of Mali distributed so much gold during his visit to Cairo that the price of the metal was devalued by as much as twenty-five percent, according to some reports. Ten years after his visit, the natives of Egypt were still talking about their royal visitor. Mansa Musa distributed so much gold that he ran out of money before his return and was forced to borrow at excessive rates of interest (up to 175 percent). Such largess was neither foolishness nor only an attempt to impress the foreigners, though he clearly did the latter. Providing handsomely for your retinue was a royal duty for an African king; supporting the poor and less fortunate was a religious duty for a Muslim. Mansa Musa was both a good ruler and a good Muslim.

Religious zeal helped motivate his actions and there is evidence that his pilgrimage strengthened his faith. Upon being told in Cairo that a Muslim should have only four wives, he asked if this also applied to kings. On being told that it did, he said, "By God, I did not know that. I renounce it [having more than four wives] from this moment."[4] The king of Mali returned home eager to strengthen education and purify Islam. He built new mosques and ordered that Friday prayers and other basic tenets of Islam be more strictly observed. He promoted Islamic scholarship and became a strong public advocate of the faith. This was both pious and wise for, according to one historian, "in return for this support accorded to Islam by the king, the whole prestige of the . . . religion was directed to exhorting loyalty to the ruler."[5] Mansa Musa clearly used his religion as a state-building force. While we cannot know his inner-most religious feelings, it is certainly true that having the Muslim ulemas [scholar-jurists] on his side would have strengthened the authority of this West African king.

A final characteristic of Mansa Musa was his concern for jus-tice, a trait he shared with his European fellow pilgrim, Louis IX. Ibn Battuta specifically mentioned the high standard of justice, order, and honesty that seemed to prevail in the Mali lands. All men, whether Muslim or not, whether black or white, were treated fairly. Theft was severely punished by death or enslavement, and there was order and prosperity in the emerging commercial centers of Niani, Timbuctu, and Gao. The city of Timbuctu, in particular, compared favorably in size, comfort, and general cultural level with many northern European cities during the fourteenth century.

The reign of Mansa Musa of Mali represents a high point in the history of traditional West African states. He brought the politi-cal structure of kingship to a high level of development and graced his kingdom with an Islamic culture and ruling class. His near-contemporary, Louis IX of France, represents a similar peak in the development of medieval Christian kingship and state-building. One standard historical reference work praises Louis of France, per-haps too grandly, as "the most chivalrous man of his age and the ideal medieval king. . . . His justice won him national support and made him the arbiter of Europe. His reign was the golden age of medieval France." Another scholar tells us that it was Louis "who was chiefly responsible for giving substance to the hitherto vague sense of identity [and] purpose . . . of the kingdom of France."[6] Louis may have been the most highly regarded monarch of me-dieval France. If he is considered "ideal," however, it is precisely because he was able to combine effectively religious piety (he was canonized a saint in 1298) with practical political measures that strengthened the royal power in France. Like Mansa Musa, he was a good ruler *and* a pious one. Unlike the African ruler, Louis IX was almost the last French king to even pretend to saintliness.

If one characteristic of medieval life was taking religion very se-riously, he most certainly was medieval. Who else but a medieval Christian would go to Mass twice a day, recite extensive prayers daily, and receive Communion six times a year, approaching the altar on his knees? If we did not know better, we would think that this man who observed a strict fast during Lent, slept in a hairshirt [a coarse, irritating haircloth undergarment worn as a form of penance for sins], and fed lepers with his own hands was a saintly hermit rather than a monarch.

But a monarch he was. The man who hated foul language and heretics also nurtured a strong dislike for barons who disobeyed him. The king who endowed religious institutions throughout the kingdom and built the beautiful Gothic chapel of Sainte Chapelle to hold a piece of the cross on which Christ was crucified also warned his son in his will to "take special care to have good bailiffs and provosts, and often to inquire of them . . . whether any of them are addicted to the vice of excessive covetousness, or untruthfulness or shifty behaviour."[7] His crusades against the infidel, launched against the advice of most of his counselors, were holy journeys that only a saintly monarch would wish to take and that only a strong one could afford.

The great crusades of the twelfth century that had established European, or "Latin," kingdoms in Palestine were long past when Louis decided to fulfill a vow and attack Egypt in the 1240s. Almost no one thought it wise to send 15,000 men in 1,800 ships across the Mediterranean—no one but Louis, who was strong enough to prevail. He had secured himself against his enemies at home for over a decade before he made the vow to "take the cross" [go on crusade wearing a garment prominently marked with a cross] in 1244.

Louis' mother, Blanche of Castile, who ruled for the young king until he was twenty, taught him the importance of keeping the royal power strong and the ways to do this. Taking advantage of the rule of a woman, French noblemen under Raymond of Toulouse led a rebellion from 1226–1231. It ended when the lords of the provinces of Brittany and Boulogne submitted and Blanche arranged a marriage between the king and Margaret of Provence to bring that land into the French kingdom. In 1242, Louis held off an attack by the English king, Henry III, and some of the feudal lords in southern France. By the end of 1243, the provinces of Aquitaine and Toulouse were under royal control. Finally, in 1259, Louis signed a treaty with the English king, giving up the two small territories of Perigord and Limousin in return for the English renunciation of all claims to the much larger areas of Normandy, Maine, and Poitou.

Securing royal power against land-hungry counts and barons was a necessary prelude to any prolonged absence from the kingdom. It was also necessary to extend royal government to new areas of France efficiently and fairly. The French legend created by Louis' biographer, Joinville, of the king sitting under an oak tree in Vincennes, distributing justice to all who approached, romantically illustrates some of the king's more practical measures: establishing clear rights of appeal from local or baronial courts; appointing *enqueteurs* [royal investigators] to report to the king any injustices perpetrated by his regular officials; selecting men of the lesser nobility as lawyers and public servants, since they would be more loyal to the king; and even staunchly refusing to allow churchmen to unduly influence his politics. Joinville is very clear on this last point. On one occasion, the French bishops asked the king to insist that his subjects who had been excommunicated do penance and return to the good graces of the church. Louis said he would do this only if the bishops would let him review each case to determine if the excommunicates had been justly kicked out of the fold in the first place. When the bishops bridled at this royal interference in church affairs, he refused to help them. The fact that Louis could combine justice and Christian duty is nicely illustrated by another story from Joinville. On his crusades, Louis objected to his troops' "consorting with prostitutes." In Egypt, he forced a knight arrested in a brothel to choose between being led bound with a rope through camp by a prostitute and giving up his horse and being dismissed from the army; the knight chose the latter.[8]

In the long run, of course, Louis IX is remembered more for his role in building the French royal state than for his two unsuccessful crusades, the second of which took his life in 1270. It is interesting that Louis regarded his faith and his holy journeys as much more important than his strengthening of French royal justice. The office of *enqueteur*, for example, was established in the years before the crusade of 1248–1254, to help him put the economic affairs of his land in order before he left for Egypt. Louis also rejected the opportunity to seize land from the English king in the 1250s because he wanted Henry to join him in the next crusade. That crusade did not get beyond Tunis, where the king died; the crusading movement itself had failed by 1291, when the last Christian stronghold in Palestine, the city of Acre, was retaken by the Muslims. Louis IX was intelligent enough to have foreseen the end; had he done so, and given up crusading on this account, he would have been less saintly. One can question whether he would have been more modern without his deep Christian faith, however, for the same faith that sent him on crusades convinced this king that he had to maintain "the rights of his subjects, the prerogatives of his crown, and the safety of his realm."[9]

Mansa Musa of Mali quite literally put his kingdom on the map. It was two years after his death in 1339 that Mali first appeared on a European map. Louis IX's medieval sense of justice and practical administrative skills helped make his kingdom one of the most powerful in Europe. Neither of these monarchs could or would have done what he did without the faith that inspires pilgrimages. Neither Mansa Musa nor St. Louis was modern, yet each enjoyed careers and prerogatives that would be the envy of many modern heads of state. What modern leader would risk being out of touch with his or her people for two to four years at a time, as these men did? Mansa Musa and Louis IX could afford their journeys, even their mistakes, because in their world kingship was sacred. If royalty had its privileges, so did divinity, and an aura of the divine surrounded medieval monarchs, both Muslim and Christian. The fact that this is no longer true is part of what makes us modern.

Notes

1. The word *Sudan,* used to describe the savanna lands that stretch across Africa south of the Sahara from coast to coast, is taken from an Arab word for black.

2. J. S. Trimingham, *A History of Islam in West Africa* (Oxford: Oxford University Press, 1962), 37.

3. Said Hamdun and Noel King, eds., *Ibn Battuta in Black Africa* (London: Rex Collings, 1975), 39, 48.

4. Trimingham, *A History of Islam in West Africa,* 71.

5. Nehemiah Levtzion, *Ancient Ghana and Mali* (New York: Holmes and Meier, 1980), 193; J. S. Trimingham, *The Influence of Islam upon Africa,* 2nd ed. (London: Longmans Group Limited, 1980), 11.

6. William L. Langer, *New Illustrated Encyclopedia of World History,* vol. I (New York: Abrams, 1975), 250–251; William Chester Jordan, *Louis IX and the Challenge of the Crusade: A Study in Rulership* (Princeton: Princeton University Press, 1979), 217.

7. Jean de Joinville, "Life of St. Louis" in *Chronicles of the Crusades,* trans. M. R. B. Shaw (Baltimore: Penguin Books, 1963), 349. Louis' Sainte Chapelle still stands in its original form, without fracture or reinforcement, after 700 years.

8. Joinville, "Life of St. Louis," pp. 177–178, 207, 292.
9. Margaret Wade Labarge, *St. Louis: Louis IX, Most Christian King of France* (Boston: Little, Brown, 1968), 249.

Further Reading

Chronicles of the Crusades, trans. M. R. B. SHAW. Baltimore: Penguin Books, 1963. Good sample of medieval historical writing and thinking.

LABARGE, MARGARET WADE. *St. Louis: Louis IX, Most Christian King of France.* Boston: Little, Brown, 1968. Readable biography.

LEVTZION, NEHEMIAH. *Ancient Ghana and Mali.* New York: Holmes and Meier, 1980. Clear, short, factual account, one of the few available.

TRIMINGHAM, J. S. *A History of Islam in West Africa.* Oxford: Oxford University Press, 1962. Good source for study of Islam south of the Sahara.

CHAPTER 12

Prince Henry and Zheng He: Sailing South

How do the structures and values of a society affect the way people view contact with other cultures? Why did Europeans benefit more from the voyages of Price Henry than the Chinese did from those of Zheng He?

It somehow doesn't seem fair. Prince Henry of Portugal (1394–1460), who was land-bound, is known to history as Henry the Navigator, while Chinese admiral Zheng He (ca. 1371–1433), who commanded fleets with hundreds of ships, is remembered as a eunuch [castrated male], if at all. Of course, Henry's personal ability to navigate—if he had any—is not what made his life significant. That Zheng He was a eunuch did not affect his ability to lead men or manage fleets. Each man is remembered as he is because of the conditions and values of his society. These conditions and values helped to determine how the Chinese and Portuguese reacted to the voyages of their remarkable explorers.

Between 1405 and 1424, the Ming dynasty ruler Yongle created a fleet and ordered it to make seven expeditions into the "Great Western Sea," or Indian Ocean. The man selected to command these voyages, the most ambitious in Chinese history, was born Ma He, a member of a Muslim family of Mongol descent in the province of Yunan. When the first Ming emperor incorporated this Mongol province into his empire in 1381, Ma He was captured, castrated, and taken to the imperial capital of Nanjing, probably to serve as a harem guard. At age twenty, Ma He entered the service of the royal prince, Zhu Di, and very soon distinguished himself as a junior officer in a civil war that brought Zhu Di to power as the Yongle emperor. The new ruler promoted Ma He to the position of superintendent of the office of eunuchs and honored him with the

Chinese surname Zheng. The new head eunuch was described as tall and handsome, with "glaring eyes, teeth as white as well-shaped shells, and a voice as loud as a huge bell," a man who "walks like a tiger and talks in a commanding voice."[1]

It was this commanding figure whom the emperor chose to lead his new fleet. In this role, Zheng He was to undertake seven voyages, each of which lasted nearly two years. On his first voyage, in 1405–1407, he commanded twenty-eight thousand men on 317 ships, many of them large "treasure ships" 400 feet long and 160 feet wide. By contrast, Columbus "discovered" America 85 years later with 120 men and a fleet of three ships, one of which was 75 feet long. The sheer size of the Ming fleet made it impossible for the Chinese to profit financially from the expedition, while Columbus' financially modest expeditions showed a profit from the first voyage.

Zheng He's first expedition traveled to India, with stops at Java and Ceylon. The fourth expedition, in 1413–1415, reached Aden and Hormuz on the Persian Gulf, and on the seventh expedition, in 1431–1433, the Chinese sent a small group to visit Mecca; they also touched the east coast of Africa as far south as Malindi near the modern state of Kenya. At each stop, Zheng He presented lavish gifts to the local rulers from "their" emperor and recorded information about interesting customs and creatures he encountered. An "Overall Survey of the Ocean's Shores Annotated" was written by Zheng He's fellow Muslim, Ma Huan; it was based on a diary that Ma Huan kept during several voyages.[2] Ma Huan's book shows the great interest the Chinese took in the dress, food, language, marriage and death rituals, and flora and fauna of the countries they visited. According to most modern historians of China, however, anthropological research was not the primary purpose of these costly trips.

There were a number of reasons the court of the Son of Heaven initiated these voyages, discounting for the moment the exuberance of a young ruler and a natural curiosity about his neighbors to the south and west. To consolidate his power won in a civil war, the emperor decided to send what the Chinese called tribute missions to all neighboring countries to set up diplomatic and economic exchanges. Owing to their advanced civilization, the Chinese, like other people before and since, believed that all other cultures were inferior and that, once foreigners became familiar with Chinese culture, they would realize it was the source of all wisdom and political power. While some representatives of foreign states felt the

Chinese claim was unwarranted, many kowtowed (bowed) before the emperor because they either regarded it as appropriate or because it enabled them to establish trade relations with the Chinese. Zheng He's voyages, then, were part of the Yongle emperor's effort to demonstrate his own power. Perhaps more important was his desire to bring money into the imperial treasury by expanding foreign trade. The voyages were also designed in part to curb Japanese piracy along the eastern coast of China, to check on possible Mongol activity in western Asia, to search for needed medicinal herbs and spices, and to overawe a few "barbarians."

Zheng He accomplished these aims in visits to at least thirty-seven countries, many more than once. At the end of his fourth voyage, in 1415, he brought back the envoys of thirty states to do homage to the Chinese emperor.[3] He also brought back a giraffe and a zebra to astonish the court; this latter creature, whose Swahili name sounded similar to the Chinese word for unicorn, was celebrated at court as a good omen for the dynasty and as an "emblem of Perfect Virtue, Perfect Government and Perfect Harmony in the Empire and in the Universe."[4] Zheng He's work had clearly boosted Ming prestige, as well as increased Chinese trade with south and west Asia.

Therefore, from a Western perspective, it is surprising that Chinese overseas voyages were abruptly halted at the end of the seventh voyage, in 1435, and were never resumed. Zheng He himself had died on this last voyage and was buried at sea. The exact date of his death, like that of his birth, is uncertain. After this, the Chinese went back to fighting nomads on the northern land frontier, something they had done for centuries. Japanese pirates soon reappeared along the southern coast. Zheng He's name lived on as the name of a Buddhist temple in Thailand and as the name of a well in Malacca.[5] In China, however, Zheng He and his travels to the "Western Ocean" were soon forgotten. A generation after his last voyage, an official in the Ministry of Defense even burned the log books of the expedition, whether deliberately or by accident, whether at the command of the emperor or on his own, no one seems to know. By 1500, it had become a capital offense to even build a boat of more than two masts, and in 1525 an edict ordered the destruction of all remaining ocean-going vessels. "In less than a hundred years the greatest navy the world had ever known had ordered itself into extinction."[6]

A far different fate awaited the work of Prince Henry of Portugal, a man who became a legend in European history. Born in 1394 as the third son of King John I and Queen Philippa of Portugal, Henry became famous as the man whose sailors explored the west coast of Africa during the first half of the fifteenth century. Every grade school student knows that, without the pioneering explorations of Prince Henry the Navigator, Bartholomeu Dias would not have been able to round the Cape of Good Hope in 1487–1488, Vasco da Gama would not have sailed to India and back in 1497–1499, and Columbus would not have sought a sea route to the Indies in 1492.

Although he never personally navigated any ships south, Henry did make it his life's work to send out ship after ship from his rocky outpost of Sagres on the Atlantic coast of Portugal. Henry either outfitted the ships himself or granted a license to private captains who would repay him with a fifth of everything valuable they brought back. In the early years, when his ships were hugging the African desert lands, Henry usually spent far more than he earned. Although his ships were much smaller than the government-built and outfitted vessels of Zheng He, Henry's record was impressive for his time and place. Men working under his direction settled in the Madeiras and discovered and settled the Azores and some of the Cape Verde Islands. In 1434, Gil Eanes finally sailed beyond Cape Bojador on the west coast of Africa after other Portuguese sailors had refused or been unable to do so on fourteen earlier trips. Many men feared sailing too far south. Current rumors included the belief that anyone passing Cape Bojador would turn black, that the sea boiled in the tropics, and that the sun's rays descended in the form of liquid fire as you approached the equator. Once the Portuguese passed Cape Bojador, a barrier more psychological than physical had been breached.

The Portuguese caravels [light, fast, maneuverable ships that could be sailed inshore] continued their journeys south in the late 1430s and 1440s. Alfonzo Goncalves Baldaia went 300 miles beyond Bojador in 1435, and in 1441 Nuno Tristao went down as far as Cape Blanco, halfway between Sagres and the equator. It was in this decade that Cape Verde was rounded, although it was not until the year of Prince Henry's death in 1460 that Pedro de Sintra reached Sierra Leone. In the early years, Henry constantly had to urge his sailors "to go back and go further." It was easier and more profitable to pirate Muslim vessels in the north than it was to take the more fearful route southwest along the barren desert coast. However, after several blacks were brought back to Portugal as slaves in 1441, the number and willingness of Henry's sailors grew. The slave trade and African exploration became intertwined, and Henry built the first European trading post used for slaves on Arguin Island in 1448.

Prince Henry did not set out to secure slaves, but the new trade in human beings did not trouble him greatly. Slaves had souls that could be saved, and that appealed to Henry as much as did the selling and "civilizing" of them. Unlike his Chinese counterpart, whose voyages had no religious aims at all, Henry had a strong desire to spread his faith and fight the infidel Moors [Muslims in northwest Africa]. Zheng He, by contrast, made no attempt to offend the religiosity of those he encountered. Personally, he offered sacrifices to a Chinese sea goddess before each voyage, but, on a tablet he placed in Ceylon in 1409 with inscriptions in Chinese, Persian, and Tamil, he offered thanks to Buddha, Allah, and the Hindu god Vishnu—all of whom were worshipped on that island. Writing such an "ecumenical" inscription would have been literally unthinkable to Henry of Portugal. Indeed, his early interest in West African exploration was stimulated by the Portuguese conquest of the Muslim city of Ceuta on the North African coast in 1415; in 1437, Henry and his brother Fernando unsuccessfully attacked the city of Tangier, near Ceuta in Muslim Morocco.

The word *crusader* has medieval associations that contrast with our image of Henry as one of the first modern explorers, but the objectives of Henry the Navigator make him a crusader in the typical Iberian fashion. A major objective of his African expeditions was to "get behind," or outflank, the Moors by sea. Like other medieval Christians, he had heard about the legendary Prester John, a Christian king in Africa somewhere south of the Sahara. If the Portuguese could reach Guinea, as they called black western Africa, they might be able to find an ally who could attack the infidel Muslims from the south. His desire to secure military allies contrasts with that of Zheng He, who sought only a formal acknowledgment of Chinese sovereignty, trade in rare goods, and political and nautical information.

Although his explorations failed to secure Henry's military and diplomatic objectives against the Moors, they provided new geographical knowledge that improved future map-making and encouraged further Portuguese exploration. They also allowed him to control many Atlantic islands, promote trade, and increase Portugal's political power at Spain's expense. In sum, Henry the Navigator's program mixed religion with economics in a way designed to appeal to the various components of Portuguese society, all of whom, unlike their Chinese counterparts, were strongly driven by the expectation of profits. His brother, King Duarte I, supported Henry's work by granting him several royal monopolies. These gave him a fifth of everything of value brought back from south of Cape Bojador and made him the "landlord" of the Madeiras, the Azores, and Cape Verde. Henry also held the monopoly on all fishing and coral gathering along the Atlantic and Mediterranean coasts of Portugal and received all fees paid by fishermen to fish in these areas. He was reputed to be the "richest man in Portugal" after the king, but he probably died in debt because of the money he spent on exploration. The Portuguese merchants supported Henry's work because of the potential profits to be gained from exploration and the slave trade. Even Portuguese pirates were pleased by the opportunity his work gave them to raid and plunder under the cover of "exploring." The Catholic Church supported Henry's missionary efforts to convert the heathen and fight the infidel, and the aristocracy generally liked both the idea of crusading and the idea of increasing Portuguese power. The loyal peasants, we must assume, enjoyed Portuguese greatness vicariously, as most peasants in most places enjoy most forms of greatness.

Because of the broad-based support for Henry's work that existed within Portuguese society, he did not need to be a navigator. One modern historian, critical of the myth of Henry as a nautical genius who ran a "school" for geographers and sailors at Sagres, put the matter quite simply: "Henry harnessed his own talents and energies to those of his family and country. He did not need to invent ships, train sailors, educate pilots or give courage to his men. He found all these at his command. What he needed to do, and what he did, was to give focus to Portuguese energies."[7]

It was the focusing of energies already there by Prince Henry of Portugal that began the "age of discovery and exploration" that we read about in our texts, while the voyages of Zheng He, the Ming admiral, remained "mere exploits."[8] We should not forget the interesting similarities between Henry and Zheng He. Both sought power for their respective rulers, though in different ways. While neither favored outright conquest of the lands he explored, both found the idea of economic domination by the "mother country" acceptable. Both had sailing vessels suitable for long ocean voyages. Yet Henry's voyages marked a beginning and those of Zheng He an ending of maritime activity. Why?

One reason this question is so intriguing is that we have the benefit of hindsight. We know what came of the voyages of Prince Henry. We know how, in the words of one of his biographers, "he set a nation's steps upon a path that led to the world's end."[9] And we know as well what happened to China—and we wonder what might have happened. Chinese vessels were not only larger but also technically superior to Western ones. Chinese sailors had the magnetic compass in the eleventh century, perhaps two centuries before their European counterparts. They also had watertight storage compartments and a "balanced rudder" that could be raised and lowered, creating greater stability. Europeans had neither of these until the late eighteenth century.[10] Given all this, it would not have been difficult for the Chinese to have dominated all of Southeast Asia, portions of India, and perhaps even the east coast of Africa.[11] There was already a substantial overseas Chinese population in Southeast Asia, and it showed every prospect of growing when the voyages were ended. If the Chinese had followed up on the voyages of Zheng He, what would the world be like today?

They did not do this, of course. Instead, China began to suffer from the intrusions of European sailors as early as the sixteenth century, just a century after Zheng He's voyages. China became prey to the West by 1850; it might have been Europe's strongest competitor. So much for speculation. What is certain is that the very structure of Chinese society in the fifteenth century made it difficult for Zheng He to be the pioneer that Henry was, even assuming that he wanted to be such a pioneer. Zheng He was a skilled administrator, diplomat, and seaman, but he was, above all, a servant of his emperor. His advancement in society depended on the emperor, not on any skills he might possess. There was little place in Ming society for a private or an independent entrepreneur [risk-taking capitalist]. Trade was a government monopoly. The Son of Heaven employed servants such as Zheng He to do his will; he would never "contract out" exploration, as the Portuguese king did.

There were also clear anti-commercial and anti-foreign biases in Chinese society during this time. The government got its money from taxes on land, not from taxing private traders and merchants. In addition, farming was considered more virtuous than business (as it was in medieval Europe until about this same time). Both Confucian and Christian ideologies glorified those who worked the land over those who soiled their hands with money. In the West, however, the diversity of states and their competition with each other, as well as the perceived need for outside goods "from the East," stimulated the rise of capitalist towns and trade after 1150. The crusades of this century also helped break down traditional biases against commerce in Europe. China was more self-sufficient and, thus, faced no real pressure to change the traditional attitude toward either trade or outsiders. Besides, some Confucian scholars felt that the very idea that China needed anything that was elsewhere, even medicinal herbs from Sumatra or Arabia, was itself demeaning.[12] The inhabitants of the Middle Kingdom (Ma Huan's translator calls it "the Central Country") did not look down upon outsiders because they were genetically programmed to do so; they did it because they could afford to; they did have a more prosperous country than their neighbors in the fifteenth century. Therefore, it is logical that the Chinese would simply view sea power as less important than maintaining a strong land army. It was. The chief threat to fifteenth-century China came from the northern barbarians; they, not Japanese or Malayan pirates, were to overrun the country in the seventeenth century. All this means that both the Chinese and the Portuguese were quite sensible in choosing the course of action they did.

Yet, given the wonderful benefit of hindsight available to historians, we can see clearly that the desire for riches of the European entrepreneurs meant that their voyages would have a much greater economic and political impact on the world than those of the Chinese, who were driven not so much by the desire for profit by by the will of one man and the immense resources of a large state. The story of these mariners and their respective countries did not play out the way anyone living in 1430 might have predicted.

Notes

1. B. Martin and S. Chien-lung, "Cheng Ho: Explorer and Navigator," in *Makers of China: Confucius to Mao* (New York: Halstead Press, 1972), 112; Louise Levathes, *When China Ruled the Seas: The Treasure Fleet of the Dragon Throne*, 1405–1433 (Oxford: Oxford University Press, 1994), 64. Cheng, although his surname, is placed first in Chinese. (The new spelling of Zheng He [pronounced "Jung Huh"] used here represents the Pinyin system of transliteration adopted by scholars only in recent years.)

2. Ma Huan, *Overall Survey of the Ocean's Shores Annotated,* edited and introduced by J. V. G. Mills (Cambridge: Cambridge University Press, 1970).
3. Jung-pang Lo, "Cheng Ho," in *Encyclopedia Britannica,* 15th ed. *Macropedia,* vol. 4 (Chicago: Macmillan, 1974), 193–194.
4. Nora C. Buckley, "The Extraordinary Voyages of Admiral Cheng Ho," History Today (July 1975): 468.
5. Ma Huan, *Overall Survey of the Ocean's Shores,* editor's introduction, 7.
6. Levathes, *When China Ruled the Seas,* 174–175.
7. Bailey W. Diffie and George D. Winius, *Foundations of the Portuguese Empire 1415–1580* (Minneapolis: University of Minnesota Press, 1977), 122.
8. Ma Huan, *Overall Survey of the Ocean's Shores,* editor's introduction, 34.
9. Elaine Sanceau, *Henry the Navigator: The Story of a Great Prince and His Times* (New York: Norton, 1947), 247.
10. Levathes, *When China Ruled the Seas,* 81–82.
11. Fernand Braudel, *Capitalism and Material Life, 1400–1800* (New York: Harper, 1973), 308, says that a Japanese junk, constructed much like those of Cheng Ho, traveled from Japan to Acapulco in 1610.
12. See Lynda Schaffer, "China, Technology, and Change," *World History Bulletin,* vol. IV (Fall, Winter 1986–1987), 1, 4–6; also Levathes, *When China Ruled the Seas,* 179–180. Paul Kennedy, *The Rise and Fall of the Great Powers: Economic Change and Military Conflict from 1500–2000* (New York: Random House, 1987), 8, notes that members of the Confucian ruling class (mandarins) distrusted merchants because they had less control over them. The mandarins hindered foreign trade by confiscating the property of merchants or banning their businesses on occasion.

Further Reading

LEVATHES, LOUISE. *When China Ruled the Seas: The Treasure Fleet of the Dragon Throne, 1405–1433.* (Oxford: Oxford University Press, 1994). This readable explanation of the career of Zheng He and his times also includes fascinating information on earlier seafaring exploits of the Chinese people.

MA HUAN. *Overall Survey of the Ocean's Shores Annotated,* edited and introduced by J. V. G. Mills. Cambridge: Cambridge University Press, 1970. This is an interesting look at what fifteenth-century Chinese thought important.

SANCEAU, ELAINE. *Henry the Navigator: The Story of a Great Prince and His Times.* New York: Norton, 1947. Flowery hero worship in places but still useful and interesting reading.

CHAPTER 13

Erasmus and Luther: The Reformer's Dilemma

To what extent is it possible to reform an institution from within? What intellectual and personal qualities led Luther to be more radical than Erasmus? Is it better to promote greater change for fewer people or less change for more people?

During the last two centuries of the European Middle Ages (1300–1500 C.E.), people took religion more seriously than most of us can imagine. Where best-selling books today give instructions on how to pay income tax, those of that day advised "on how to escape Hell."[1] This world, into which Desiderius Erasmus (1466–1536) and Martin Luther (1483–1546) were born, was one in which both Heaven and Hell seemed much closer to people than they do today. One reason was that life was shorter and more precarious for most people than it is for us.

Men and women heard stories of the Black Death, a plague that had carried off one-third of the population in many parts of Europe in 1348–1349 and that occasionally reappeared. They also knew wars and famines that periodically swept through the countryside. Even princes and merchants gained and lost fortunes during these years as men fought to get their share of the new wealth coming from the East. The Christian church, too, had to respond to this change and uncertainty. No longer as politically powerful as it had been in the thirteenth century, the church could no longer dominate kings and princes as it once had. And it could do little to control the plague or the economy. It could, however, take advantage of the people's longing for salvation.

While Christian leaders found it difficult to explain why God had sent disease to bedevil men and women, they continued to comfort people with various forms of external piety to make them feel closer to God as they faced death from plagues, wars, and famines. Medieval Christians could assure themselves of God's favor (grace) and keep themselves in a "state of grace" (the opposite of a "state of sin") by undertaking good actions, most of which cost time, money, or both. Clergymen encouraged the faithful to go on pilgrimages to holy places, usually shrines of saints, such as that of Thomas Becket in Canterbury. Some princes and bishops also collected relics, usually portions of the bones or clothing of saintly people, which they were willing to allow people to view for a price. People could also pay a priest to say Masses for the salvation of their souls. Finally, one could receive an "indulgence," the remission of punishment for past sins, in exchange for specified prayers and/or an offering of money to support a good cause. Indulgences could help a person escape all punishment for sins (in Purgatory) and go straight to Heaven after he or she died.

All these good works gave some comfort to those desperate for tangible evidence of earned "grace." They also helped enrich the institutional church that controlled their distribution. This "good works" theology, and the political power of the institutional church which lay behind it, offended the spiritual sensitivities of men like Erasmus and Luther who saw Christianity as a matter of inner devotion to Christ, and not primarily a matter of good works. These men, along with others, believed the church sorely needed reform.

And it was reform of the church that they accomplished, though hardly in the way either preferred or imagined. Martin Luther sparked the famous sixteenth-century Reformation in 1517, when he wrote his famous list of "Ninety-five Theses," explaining errors in the church's policy on indulgences as preached by German Dominican priest Johan Tetzel. In this statement, Luther asserted that God's free grace and not human works was responsible for our salvation. Luther was influenced by others, among them Desiderius Erasmus, a Christian humanist who suggested that true religion was much simpler and more scriptural than the official church seemed to believe. After 1516, Luther prepared his university lectures and sermons using a copy of the Greek New Testament edited by Erasmus, whom he admired. By the mid-1520s, as the Reformation began to divide most of Europe politically and religiously, it was said that "Erasmus laid the egg that Luther hatched," meaning that Luther was merely taking to their logical conclusion some of the ideas of Erasmus. Erasmus denied this and, despite his early defense of

Luther and his ideas, refused to reject the authority of the Roman Church. Luther, by contrast, did respect that authority, was excommunicated by the pope in 1520, and, in an act of public defiance, burned the letter of excommunication.

Both Erasmus and Luther were men who wished to improve the institutional church and the spiritual lives of its members. Their disagreements with each other—Erasmus deplored Luther's "violence" and the "tragedy" of a divided Christendom, while Luther denounced Erasmus as a coward and pagan who did not *really* understand Scripture after all—highlight the reformer's dilemma. Is it better to seek change from within an institution, even if you are likely to get less change that way? Or is it better to act boldly and accept the risk of getting kicked out, as Luther was willing to do by 1520, in order to preserve your integrity and the opportunity to make more significant reforms? Is it better to promote greater change for fewer people, or less change for more people? Luther chose the first option, Erasmus the second. Their personal histories help explain their decisions.

By his own account, Erasmus of Rotterdam was born the bastard child of a priest on October 27, 1466.[2] Despite the circumstances of his birth, his parents cared for him well until their deaths from the plague when he was about fourteen. During his early years, Erasmus received a humanistic education at a monastic school in the Netherlands which stressed inward spirituality and devotion to Christ more than doctrine or dogma. This emphasis would remain a part of Erasmus' "Christian philosophy" throughout his life.[3]

Erasmus entered an Augustinian monastery at Steyn in 1487. Later he claimed he was ill with fever at the time and was "duped" into believing he could seriously pursue scholarship in the monastery. Erasmus took the religious vows of poverty, chastity, and obedience and was ordained a priest in 1492. He took the first opportunity, however, to leave the monastery, worked as secretary to the bishop of Cambrai for several years, and in 1495 began work on a doctor's degree in theology at the University of Paris.[4] While in Paris, Erasmus found, as Luther did later, that he disliked the irrelevant "how-many-angels-can-sit-on-the-head-of-a-pin" sort of questions that preoccupied many scholastic medieval theologians. He did find himself attracted to the study of the ancient Greek and Roman virtues promoted by a group known as humanists. These scholars were part of the intellectual move-ment known as the Renaissance, one which revived interest in classical learning in Europe between 1300 and 1700. During his student years in Paris and a visit in 1499 to England, where he met famous Renaissance humanists John Colet and Thomas More, Erasmus evolved a synthesis of classical virtue and Christian piety which he felt could be used to reform the lives of individual Christians and thereby the church itself. From such pagan authors as Cicero he took the virtues of *humanitas* (love of humankind based on a belief in the dignity of the human being as a rational creature) and *concordia* (a rational harmonizing of conflicting viewpoints). From Christian writers such as Jerome and from Scripture, Erasmus took the virtues of compassion, patience, forgiveness, humility, and love.[5]

Armed with his new convictions about the relationship between holiness and "good letters," or scholarship, Erasmus began to promote his beliefs. In an early work, *The Handbook of the Christian Soldier*, written in 1501, Erasmus argued that accurate knowledge of Scripture was extremely important to a Christian and that religion was primarily a matter of inward devotions, love of God and neighbor. In his witty, direct, but abrasive style, Erasmus wrote:

> You venerate saints; you are glad to touch their relics. But you condemn what good they have left, namely the example of a pure life. . . . You wish to deserve well of Peter and Paul? Imitate the faith of one, the charity of the other—and you will . . . do more than if you were to dash back and forth to Rome ten times. . . .[6]

To make the new learning possible for more Christians, Erasmus spent several years learning Greek in order to construct an improved edition of the New Testament from available manuscripts. This work, published in 1516, included a preface in which he wrote enthusiastically about his hope that someday God's word would be available to all. Christ's teachings were simple enough, he believed, that all men and women should have access to them in their own languages. "We embellish a wooden or stone statue with gems and gold for the love of Christ. Why not, rather, mark with gold and gems . . . these writings which bring Christ to us so much more effectively than any paltry image?"[7]

While some considered these judgments of Erasmus, by now a famous scholar, irreverent and perhaps even heretical, his attacks on the misuse of power by church men, their exaggeration of the trivial, and their ignorance, were continuous and very deliberate. In his commentary on the New Testament, he occasionally stretched a point to make the text apply "to the familiar targets of his criticism, the corruption of the clergy, the ignorance of the theologians . . . empty ceremonies, vows, penance, relics, and monasticism." Perhaps even more subversive was a satire which Erasmus wrote anonymously in 1513, *Julius Exclusus*. In this work, the warrior-pope Julius II is excluded from Heaven by St. Peter because, instead of teaching "true doctrine," he has made the church "splendid with regal palaces, splendid horses and mules, troops of servants, armies, officers . . . glamorous prostitutes and obsequious pimps."[8]

Given the tone of many of Erasmus' criticisms of the church, it is not surprising that people would expect the Dutch humanist to be an early and enthusiastic supporter of German reformer Martin Luther, since Luther and Erasmus criticized many of the same abuses. Such was not the case. From the beginning, Erasmus' support of Luther was hesitant and qualified; it soon turned to bitter disappointment. To understand why this happened we must understand that Luther's attack on the church came from a theological rather than a humanistic direction. "Erasmus was concerned about ignorance, Luther about sin," one author wrote.[9] The fact that Luther changed forever the religious map of Europe shows which of the two concerns most sixteenth-century believers took more seriously.

Not only sin, but life itself, was serious for the Saxon mining family into which Luther was born in 1483. His parents were strict and his early religious training a mixture of traditional piety and half-pagan beliefs in gnomes, fairies, sprites, and witches.[10] Like Erasmus, Luther had a sensitive soul but grew up in a far less cosmopolitan environment. Perhaps it was to be expected that the young Luther, despite acquiring great learning in his later years, would spend many years seeking to be certain he was worthy of salvation.

For more than fifteen years, Martin Luther sought that certainty of salvation by living as an Augustinian monk, a priest and a teacher in the Saxon towns of Erfurt and Wittenberg. Luther was bright and energetic as well as earnest; he advanced far more rapidly than most after entering the cloister [monastic house] in Erfurt in the summer of 1505. Two years later, he was ordained a priest, and five years after that, in 1512, he was made a Doctor of Theology, an honor usually given only those in their forties or older. By this time, Luther was professor of Bible at the University of Wittenberg. One of his regular responsibilities was to preach and lecture to his colleagues in the cloister as well as to students. While preparing lectures on the Psalms and Paul's Epistle to the Romans, Luther experienced his great insight about faith.

Since he took his faith very seriously, Luther had been troubled for years by the feeling that, no matter how hard he tried, no matter how carefully he performed his religious duties or confessed his sins, God remained angry at him. Luther struggled during these years to accept the fact that God did indeed love him. Sometime between 1512 and 1517, Luther had a "conversion experience." While reading Paul's words in the Epistle to the Romans, "the righteous shall live by faith," Luther became convinced that nothing men or women can do can earn them salvation. People are saved by "faith alone" and not by any good or pious works.[11] This would become a central insight of the Protestant Reformation.

It was this basic insight, and the trust in Scripture which made it credible for him, which gave Luther the courage to walk the road to Reformation. The first step on this road was the 1517 writing of the theses against doctrinal errors associated with the practice of granting indulgences. Though hindsight calls this the beginning of the Reformation, it was not immediately dramatic. More important were the events of the next four years: his debate with theologian Johann Eck in 1519 in Leipzig, in which he denied the authority of the pope when it conflicted with Scripture; the pope's excommunication of him in 1520; and the meeting of the German princes at Worms in 1521, at which time he refused to deny his teachings and was declared an outlaw.

In addition, during the year 1520, Luther wrote three essays which, taken together, defined the major principles of Protestant, or Reformed, Christianity. In his *Address to the German Nobility*, Luther challenged the authority of the Roman pope in particular and the status of the clergy in general; he declared his belief in the priesthood of all believers. In *The Babylonian Captivity of the Church*, he attacked the sacraments as, for the most part, good works unjustified in Scripture. Eventually, Luther and the Protestants reduced the sacraments to two, Baptism and Eucharist (Communion). Finally, in *The Freedom of the Christian,* Luther expressed his belief in salvation by faith. When the Elector of Saxony, Luther's prince, decided to protect him against the agents of the German emperor in 1521, it became clear that this theological rift had political overtones which might make it far less easy to heal than was apparent in 1517.

Back in Louvain [today in Belgium but then in the Netherlands] Erasmus was beginning to worry. He understood from the beginning of Luther's attack on indulgences that the German friar shared his dislike of external piety. Erasmus, however, disliked Luther's wholesale attack on church authority and his often strident language. (Luther called the Roman pope the "whore of Babylon" and the Antichrist.) In a letter to Luther in May 1519, Erasmus suggested that "more can be accomplished by polite restraint than by vehemence." He also believed that "it is more advisable to scream out against those who abuse papal authority than against the popes themselves." To a mutual friend, however, Erasmus expressed his general support of Luther. "I pray," he wrote in July 1520, "that the supreme and wonderful Christ will so temper Luther's pen that he can be of very great profit to evangelical piety. . . . [Among] Luther's opponents I see many men who breathe the spirit of the world rather than of Christ."[12]

Erasmus' qualified support for Luther from 1519 to 1521 was based on their shared dislike of abuses and on the behavior of Luther's enemies. Luther challenged the Roman officials with Scripture. They responded with authority: you cannot possibly be right because we have power and tradition on our side; if you do not recant, we will excommunicate you; we are not interested in the reasons for your position, just in whether or not you will stubbornly persist in holding to it. Writing to one of Luther's enemies, the Archbishop of Mainz, in 1519, Erasmus said that "if [Luther] is innocent, I do not want him crushed by a faction of rogues, and if he is in error, I wish him to be corrected, not destroyed. This approach agrees better with the example of Christ." A year later, in November 1520, Erasmus met with Luther's prince, Frederick of Saxony, in Cologne. Frederick had asked for Erasmus' advice on the Luther question prior to the meeting with the emperor (Diet of Worms) to be held the following spring. Erasmus wrote a list of statements, or axioms, as guidance for Frederick. They suggested that the attack on Luther was caused "by the hatred of letters" and the "desire for supremacy." Erasmus added that those "closest to the Gospel teaching are said to be the least offended by Luther"; he noted that "this affair" should "be settled by the mature deliberation of serious and impartial men."[13]

But this would not happen. The papal letter condemning Luther was so violent that both Luther and Erasmus questioned whether it really came from the pope. It had. The declaration of the Diet of Worms making Luther an outlaw soon divided the German princes into two camps. In 1520 Erasmus wrote prophetically: "The case is tending toward a greater crisis than certain men suppose." In succeeding years, he continued to lament the "dangerous dissension" and the "tragedy" of the Luther affair. Several times he referred to the "bitter medicine" of Luther, which, if swallowed, might produce good health in the church.[14]

For Erasmus, the tragedy rapidly became a personal one. He was caught in the middle, with both sides insistently urging him to speak out on their behalf. For several years, he continued to write critically about abuses in the church but refused to "join" the reformers in Germany or elsewhere because he believed one could correct abuses without leaving the Roman church. One did not have to attack papal authority, for example, in order to reform one's personal religious life in accord with the dictates of Scripture. Finally, in 1524, Erasmus did attack Luther's belief that the human will was so corrupted that without grace one could not do anything meritorious. To Erasmus' *Diatribe on the Freedom of the Will*, Luther responded in 1525 with his *On the Enslaved Will*. Although both men "talked past one another" in this debate, with each misunderstanding or exaggerating the views of the other, the exchange does illustrate the fundamental differences between the two reformers. Luther, in one of his extravagant and violent moods when he responded to the Dutch humanist, called him "a babbler, a skeptic, an Epicurean hog—stupid, hypocritical, and ignorant of Scripture."[15] There were clear temperamental differences separating these two reformers. Erasmus was a quiet scholar who could see nothing to be gained by shouting. Twice during these years, he changed residences when the political temperature got too hot. He left Louvain for Basel, Switzerland, in 1521 because of the anti-Luther sentiment in Louvain. The tumult of the Reformation in Basel drove him from that city in 1529 for five years. "I have seriously and openly discouraged violence," Erasmus wrote in 1524 to his friend and Luther's close associate, Philip Melanchthon. "Even if I were an ardent devotee of the papist faction, I would still oppose violence, because that path only leads to more violence."[16] He was right, and there is nothing in his life to suggest he was not absolutely sincere on this point.

However, there were also more than temperamental differences separating Erasmus and Luther—and these Erasmus did not fully understand. As early as 1517, after receiving Erasmus' New Testament translation, Luther wrote to a colleague that he was suspicious of Erasmus' love of pagan learning. "I am afraid . . . that he does not advance the cause of Christ and grace of God sufficiently." That Erasmus seemed to put knowledge above grace continued to bother Luther in later years and shows up clearly in the debate on free will.[17] Luther correctly saw the differences between himself and Erasmus as theological. In the words of Roland Bainton, the biographer of both men, they simply had different concepts of salvation: "this for Luther consisted in the forgiveness of sins by a sheer act of God's grace, for Erasmus in fellowship with God calling for a human response."[18]

Given this difference, all of Erasmus' talk about Luther's enemies really being enemies of "good learning," a theme that runs through Erasmus' letters, is beside the point. So, too, is Erasmus' belief that, if only Luther and the Papists would lower their voices and talk reasonably about the self-evident truth of Scripture, the differences could be ironed out. Luther could not have done this, even if he had been a calmer person less given to abusive language. His God was simply not the one Erasmus worshipped. His God was a demanding one, not interested in the rational moderation stressed by many humanists. In the words of Bainton again, "the God of Luther, as of Moses, was the God who inhabits the storm clouds and rides on the wings of the wind. At his nod the earth trembles, and the people before him are as a drop in the bucket. He is a God of majesty and power."[19] It is ironic that despite his differences with Erasmus, his strong language and clear resentment of Roman abuses, Luther did not see himself as a German nationalist and did not really want to divide the church. He called for "repentance and renewal" and was like Erasmus in simply wanting people to live virtuous lives based on Scripture.[20]

However, the work of Martin Luther and, after him, John Calvin and others, did bring about major changes in the Christian church. The Catholic bishops at the Council of Trent (1545–1563) re-asserted their basic doctrines and made no attempt to accommo-date the ideas of the reformers. Before long, Western Christendom was fragmented into hundreds of denominations and sects. At-tempts to restore unity in dozens of bloody religious wars failed as Catholics and Protestants rejected the muted calls for a measure of mutual tolerance. It was common in that day to prove your love of God by hatred of your "heretic" or "Papist" neighbor. It is only in our own day, a more ecumenical one, that some people have begun to better understand the real aims of both Erasmus and Luther and ask "what if . . . ?"

Notes

1. Roland H. Bainton, *Here I Stand: A Life of Martin Luther* (Nashville: Abingdon Press, 1950), 29.
2. Desiderius Erasmus, *Christian Humanism and the Reformation: Selected Writings,* ed. John C. Olin (New York: Harper and Row, 1965), 23–25.
3. Ibid.; Roland H. Bainton, *Erasmus of Christendom* (New York: Charles Scribner's Sons, 1969), 8–11.
4. Erasmus, *Christian Humanism,* 26–27; J. Kelley Sowards, *Desiderius Erasmus* (Boston: Twayne Publishers, 1975), 4–9.
5. Bainton, *Erasmus,* 41–43, 113–114; Johan Huizinga, *Erasmus and the Age of the Reformation* (New York: Harper and Row, 1957), 102–103; E. Harris Harbison, *The Christian Scholar in the Age of the Reformation* (New York: Scribner's Sons, 1956), 70–77.
6. Erasmus, *Christian Humanism,* 7–9.
7. Ibid., 96–100, 106.
8. Sowards, *Erasmus,* 35–36, 88; Bainton, *Erasmus,* 106–109.
9. P. S. Allen, *Erasmus* (Oxford: Oxford University Press, 1934), quoted in Harbison, *Christian Scholar,* 110.
10. Bainton, *Here I Stand,* 22–23, 25–27.
11. John M. Todd, *Luther: A Life* (New York: Crossroad Publishing Co., 1982), 72–79; Bainton, *Here I Stand,* 60–66.
12. *Erasmus and His Age: Selected Letters of Desiderius Erasmus,* ed. Hans J. Hillerbrand, trans. Marcus A. Haworth, S. J. (New York: Harper and Row, 1970), 141, 149.
13. Erasmus, *Christian Humanism,* 138–139; 146–149.
14. Ibid.; *Erasmus and His Age: Selected Letters,* 153, 163, 177, 182; Bainton, *Erasmus,* 160.
15. Bainton, *Erasmus,* 187–190; Sowards, *Erasmus,* 103; one German theolo-gian put Luther's position on free will (and, indeed, the general

Protestant one) very succinctly when he wrote: "The central point of Luther's argument lies not in the question of whether man has the ability to do what he wishes, but rather in the question of whether he can do what he should." See Werner Elert, *Morphologie des Luthertums* (Munich: Beck, 1931), I, 22, quoted in G. C. Berkouwer, *Conflict Met Rome* (Kampen: J. H. Kok, 1948), 149.

16. *Erasmus and His Age,* 176.
17. *Luther's Works,* vol. 48, *Letters I,* ed., trans. Gottfried Krodel (Philadelphia: Fortress Press, 1963), 40, 53; see vol. 49, *Letters II* (Philadelphia: Fortress Press, 1972), 44.
18. Bainton, *Erasmus,* 192.
19. Bainton, *Here I Stand,* 385.
20. See Heiko Oberman, *Luther: Man Between God and the Devil,* trans. Eileen Walliser-Schwarzbart (New Haven: Yale University Press, 1989), 12, 44–46, 49, 64, 205.

Further Reading

BAINTON, ROLAND H. *Here I Stand: A Life of Martin Luther.* Nashville: Abingdon, 1950. Old standard work, very well done.

Erasmus and His Age: Selected Letters of Desiderius Erasmus, ed. HANS J. HILLERBRAND, trans. MARCUS A. HAWORTH, S. J. New York: Harper and Row, 1970. Gives reader a good look at the personality of Erasmus.

HUIZINGA, JOHAN. *Erasmus and the Age of the Reformation.* New York: Harper and Row, 1957. Sympathetic account by a fellow countryman.

TODD, JOHN M. *Luther: A Life.* New York: Crossroad Publishing Co., 1982. Thoughtful, fair work by a Roman Catholic.

CHAPTER 14

Elizabeth and Akbar: The Religion of the Ruler?

Can a ruler use religious conflict to strengthen his or her own rule? Can a ruler's religious preference be the basis of unity in a religiously divided state?

It seemed like a great idea at the time. In 1530 Catholic and Lutheran negotiators devised what they thought was a simple plan to end the first of many European religious wars that accompanied the Reformation begun by Martin Luther. It was the Latin phrase "cuius regio, eius religio" ("the religion of the prince is the religion of the people"). These key words of the peace treaty of Augsburg meant that the religion of the ruler would be the only official religion in the ruler's land. If your prince was Lutheran, all churches in your state became Lutheran, and any who wished to remain Catholic had to pack up and move to the nearest state with a Catholic ruler. The reverse was true, of course, if your ruler was Catholic and you were Lutheran.

While this political response to religious conflict was flawed (What if you were neither a Lutheran nor a Catholic but a follower of John Calvin?), it did illustrate the problems faced by rulers in religiously divided states in the sixteenth century. And the political problems posed by religious divisions were not limited to Europe. Muslim armies had swept as far east as western China and south into northwestern India as early as the eighth century. By the late twelfth century, central Asian Turks had established the Delhi Sultanate, a Muslim-dominated state in the northern heartland of the Hindu subcontinent of India, and one in which the native Hindus faced much discrimination.

How important, then, was "the religion of the prince" in the tumultuous sixteenth century? Two major rulers, Queen Elizabeth I of England (1533–1603) and Emperor Abu-ul-Fath Jalal-ud-Din Muhammad Akbar of Mughal India (1534–1606), give us the opportunity to answer this question. Both consciously tried to create what we might call a hybrid religion as a way of promoting social stability and loyalty to the ruler in their divided states. Elizabeth, daughter of King Henry VIII and Anne Boleyn, came to the throne determined to bring religious peace to a country which had experienced years of sometimes violent changes. Although Henry VIII broke with the Roman church in 1532 in order to divorce Queen Catherine and marry Elizabeth's mother, he did not become a Lutheran. He wanted England to remain Catholic, with himself in charge of the English Church. He persecuted Lutherans and other Protestants until his death in 1547. For the next ten years, Elizabeth's half-brother, Edward VI (reigned 1547–1553), and half-sister, Mary (r. 1553–1558), took England on a dizzying religious ride. Edward and his advisors wanted the Church of England to be as much like Protestant churches as possible, while Mary (daughter of Henry's first wife, Catholic Queen Catherine of Aragon) officially returned England to the Catholic fold, executing some 300 Protestants as heretics in the process. Akbar (the name means "Great") faced the task of consolidating and expanding the Mughal Empire, which his father, Humayun, had lost and only partially regained before his untimely death. Unlike other Muslim rulers of India who looked down upon most non-Muslims as pagans or infidels, Akbar came to believe that a state policy of "universal peace," which accepted and appreciated the many different faiths of India (Hindus, Jains, Shia and Sunni Muslims, Zoroastrians [called Parsees in India] and Christians), was the best way to promote loyalty to the ruler.

Both Elizabeth and Akbar had weapons other than religion to control their subjects. Akbar's military skills were considerable and his conquest and rule of northern India from coast to coast was aided by an elaborate system of administration and revenue collection. Elizabeth used her cunning, energy, and intelligence to control friends and enemies alike. She also had a strong base of popular support, which she manipulated to her advantage. Both Elizabeth and Akbar were successful leaders who laid the foundation for the greatness of their respective states. They are generally seen by historians as having that special "something extra, that flash of the eye or turn of the head, which marks the crossing of the gulf between ability and genius."[1] The extent to which the religious policies of Elizabeth and Akbar promoted unity in their respective states is a complicated question. Historians disagree, especially in their evaluation of the policy of Akbar, and it is clear that neither ruler got exactly what he or she wanted. A look at the careers of these colorful and powerful sixteenth-century leaders can help us better understand their strengths and weaknesses as we attempt to answer the questions posed at the beginning of this essay.

Religion was an issue for Elizabeth from the moment of her birth, which made her the Protestant heir to the throne in place of her Catholic sister, Mary. Her position changed suddenly when she was three; her mother, Anne, was declared a traitor and sent to the block [beheaded], and Elizabeth joined her sister, Mary, in being officially declared a bastard by a law of 1536. Despite this turn of events, Elizabeth was taught to love and honor her father as the king. She spent her early years pleasantly enough with Katherine Parr, Henry's last wife. Katherine brought all of Henry's children together as a family and saw to their education. Elizabeth received a classical education and could read Greek and Latin and speak French, Italian, and Spanish well enough to conduct business with ambassadors from those countries in their own languages. In 1547, shortly after Henry's death, Katherine married Thomas Seymour, and Elizabeth lived with them, experiencing some unwelcome sexual advances from Seymour when she was fourteen. When Katherine died in childbirth in 1548, Seymour wished to marry Elizabeth—by then living elsewhere—but she "replied evasively," a skill she refined in future years.[2] Because of Seymour's intrigues against the government of Edward VI, Elizabeth was briefly viewed with suspicion. She was in much greater danger after 1553 when her sister, Mary, became queen and some members of her household implicated her in some Protestant plots against the new Catholic queen. Elizabeth responded by meeting with Mary, declaring her wish to become Catholic, and asking her sister to send her some vestments, crucifixes, and other Mass "gear" to use in her private chapel. Elizabeth was placed under guard in the Tower of London prison for a time, and many of Mary's advisors wanted her put to death as an enemy of the state. Interestingly, it was Mary's husband, Spanish King Philip II, who protected Elizabeth, something she always remembered, even years later when their countries were at war.[3]

Mary, like her half-brother, Edward, died after a short reign, and Elizabeth became queen on November 17, 1558. Even though her background as the "bastard" daughter of Anne Boleyn seemed to make it a foregone conclusion that she would restore Protestant Christianity as the official religion of England, one of Elizabeth's biographers points out that she could have left England a Catholic country. After all, many English subjects accepted Mary's return to the Catholic fold, and Elizabeth had professed to be a Roman Catholic for five years. Nevertheless, Elizabeth created a "Religious Settlement" in 1559 that made England a Protestant country because (1) she had been raised as a Protestant and was a sincere believer and (2) she would be accepted as the legitimate monarch by Catholics but would be supported more fervently as the "only hope" of the many Protestants, since the next in line to be ruler was Roman Catholic Mary Stuart, Queen of the Scots and Elizabeth's cousin.[4]

Elizabeth's "Religious Settlement," approved by the English Parliament within six months of her coronation, created what we know today as the "Church of England" or (outside of England today) the "Protestant Episcopal" Church. Like the Lutheran Churches in Germany, it was a state church and Elizabeth was declared the "Supreme Governor" of the church.[5] All clergy had to take an oath recognizing the queen's position and promising to "renounce and forsake all foreign jurisdiction . . . and authorities [the Pope] and bear true faith and allegiance to the queen's highness" and to her successors. Parliament also passed, in addition to this "Act of Supremacy," an important "Act of Uniformity." This restored Protestant forms of worship, ratified Elizabeth's earlier decision to put most of the worship service in English, and provided penalties for churchmen who refused to accept these measures and fines for laypeople who refused to attend Sunday services.[6]

Elizabeth's church still looked like the "Catholic" Church of her father's day. It had bishops and priests instead of the ministers and elders used by Calvinists, and they were required by law to wear clerical garb at church services. Churches still had crucifixes, the queen kept candles in her private chapel, and she issued orders retaining stained glass windows and other "popish" elements in churches, even though these were hated by the Calvinists, or "Puritans." The Puritans not only wished a church "purified" of all Roman Catholic ritual and theology but they also wanted a state church which would control, with firm punishments, what people believed, how they worshipped, and all forms of "manners and moral." Elizabeth believed this strict of a policy could lead to a religious civil war in England.[7] Instead, the queen tried to create a church that had, both in appearance and doctrine, "a distinctive character of its own—neither Lutheran, Roman Catholic, nor Reformed [Calvinist or Presbyterian]." In 1563, she supported a group of moderate bishops who drew up a statement of beliefs, the Thirty-nine Articles. This contained many beliefs Catholics could have accepted, some which Lutherans and Calvinists could accept; it remained deliberately ambiguous on controversial issues such as the exact nature of Predestination and the question of whether or not Christ was really present in the Sacrament of the Eucharist.[8] Elizabeth was a sincere Protestant but not a person given to deep theological reflection. She once told the Catholic French ambassador that "there was only one Jesus Christ and one faith, all the rest they disputed about were trifles."[9] Her main concern was religious peace and the unity of her kingdom, not theological subtleties. If English subjects would show their loyalty to God and country by attending church on Sunday, and thereby accept the queen as "the only regulator of public worship and church government,"[10] she did not care much what people said or did in the privacy of their homes.

Elizabeth was not mistaken in fearing the political divisiveness of religion. During her reign, the neighboring country of France was torn apart by religious wars between Catholics and Protestants (Huguenots). The German states and the Netherlands remained divided religiously, and Catholic Spanish King Philip II, her former brother-in-law, was being urged by the pope to undertake a crusade against Protestant England. Elizabeth herself was officially "excommunicated" by the pope in 1570 during one of the several unsuccessful plots against her throne by those who wished to make her cousin, Mary Queen of Scots, the next queen of England.

Given these foreign and domestic threats, it was understandable that Elizabeth would follow a religious policy designed to prevent persecution of Catholics by zealous Protestants in part because she did not want to give Catholic Spain an excuse to attack her. Unlike her sister, Mary, she went out of her way to avoid sending people to the stake for their religious views, even though she was quite firm with any person or group that questioned her royal authority.

When Parliament (which contained many members favorable to Puritanism) passed a law in 1563 stating that any person who twice refused to take the oath recognizing the queen's supremacy over the church was to be executed, Elizabeth instructed Matthew Parker, the Archbishop of Canterbury, to be sure that no one was asked to take the oath more than once.[11] The wisdom of Elizabeth's policy was shown in 1588, when the Spanish sent a massive armada of ships to invade England in hopes of returning England to the Catholic fold. Catholics supported Elizabeth in this moment of national peril; there was no uprising of Catholics to overthrow their Protestant ruler. The Spanish were prevented from landing by the skillful work of English sailors and a timely storm that the English referred to as "a Protestant wind." Although Catholic priests were sent to England to secretly celebrate Mass and administer Sacraments to English Catholics and although over a hundred of these men were executed for treason, most English Catholics remained loyal to the queen, and the total number of Catholics declined during her reign. Elizabeth was also willing to deal harshly with Protestant critics of her policy. Two Dutch Anabaptists attending an illegal prayer meeting in 1575 were judged guilty of heresy for denying that a Christian could be a government official, and they were burned at the stake. And, in 1579, when a lawyer named John Stubbs wrote a work attacking the French royal family and the queen's proposed marriage to the French Catholic Duke of Anjou, she ordered that his right hand be cut off with a meat cleaver. It was said that, after his hand was severed at the wrist, he lifted his hat with his left hand and shouted, "God save the queen" before he fainted.[12] Elizabeth often used marriage negotiations as a diplomatic tool; some believed that she might have married the duke if there had not been such strong objections to this match with a Catholic foreigner.

Her religious policy was not the only reason Elizabeth is fondly remembered and has an era named after her. We speak of "Elizabethan England" because this queen ruled for forty-four years and was able to develop and use her skills as a ruler and a woman to create a strong sense of personal loyalty in her subjects. She had excellent advisors and adventuresome servants, such as Sir Walter Raleigh and Sir Francis Drake, who established England as a strong naval power, The queen also learned early in her reign that she could maintain her control by meeting with her councilors individually and by asking them for their individual views in writing. Hot-tempered at times, she was known to even slap her courtiers and order them out of her presence. Members of Parliament whose speeches displeased her were sent to prison. Yet she always released them, as she nearly always restored unlucky courtiers to "her favor" by inviting them back to court. This was a person "in which the spontaneous outburst of a high-tempered woman blended with the artifices of a calculating politician."[13] Although Elizabeth was doubtless difficult to work with, she certainly understood how to appeal to her subjects. Each year she moved her court around the country on her colorful "progresses," visiting the homes of her nobles, letting the people see her and entertain her with plays, speeches of praise, and poetry. These journeys allowed people to see their queen in person, as she gratefully acknowledged their devotion. She also used her position as a woman to strengthen this loyalty. Historians disagree on why Elizabeth never married, but, whatever her reason, she did deliberately create the impression among ordinary people that she cared more about them than about having a husband; she could be seen as "married" to England. On the eve of the anticipated Spanish invasion, when the armada had already entered the English channel, Elizabeth visited some of her troops and made one of the most famous speeches in English history, saying, "I know I have the body of a weak and feeble woman, but I have the heart and stomach of a king, and of a king of England too! And [I] think foul scorn that Parma [Spanish general] or Spain, or any prince of Europe, should dare to invade the borders of my realm!" The people loved it; perhaps in that moment she became the "good Queen Bess" remembered fondly by generations of English people.[14]

Since Mughal Emperor Akbar lived in a place so distant and different from Elizabeth's England, it is unusual to find any similarities between the two rulers beyond the dates of their reigns. Yet Akbar, like Elizabeth, experienced a troubled youth, marked by an awareness of religious differences. Descended from the great Mongol and Turkish conquerors Genghis Khan and Tamerlane, he was born in the house of a Hindu ruler, while his father was on the run, trying to recapture land in northeast India. Akbar's father was a Sunni Muslim, while his mother was a Shiite [two large, theologically different branches of Islam]. His tutor, Abul Latif, taught him the principle of "universal peace," which encouraged tolerance of all religions. While growing up, he was captured and rescued three times as his father and uncles fought for control of the empire. While these struggles were over family inheritance and not over religious issues, it was clear to the young prince that the support of Muslim scholars or holy men (ulema) could help a ruler gain popular support; it was also clear to the young Akbar that anyone who would successfully rule India would have to deal with the fact that most of his subjects would not be Muslims. When his father, Humayun, died in 1556, Akbar was only thirteen. The empire was ruled in Akbar's name by a regent, Bairam Khan, a Shiite Muslim who successfully completed the conquests of much of what is today Pakistan and Afghanistan. Bairam Khan's increasingly arrogant decisions and lavish living led Akbar to replace the regent and begin to rule in his own right in 1560.[15]

The young man who would expand the Mughal Empire to its greatest extent has been described as a broad-shouldered person of "uncommon dignity," with long hair, a loud voice of "peculiar richness," "bright and flashing eyes," and a "powerful, magnetic, and inspiring" personality.[16] Historians have also been impressed by the seeming contradictions in Akbar's personality. Akbar was a deeply spiritual man but also a brutal warrior. He said that "a monarch should be ever intent on conquest, otherwise his neighbors rise in arms against him," yet, when not fighting, he loved to engage in theological and philosophical discussions with learned men from many religions. He loved hunting but spent many years as a virtual vegetarian. He "spent whole nights repeating the name of the Almighty God," had mystical experiences, and went on pilgrimages. Yet this same man authorized the massacre of thousands of people, many of them women and children, after conquering the Hindu fortress of Chitor, and he ordered the building of a mound made from the heads of his fallen enemies after the battle of Panipat in 1556. Akbar could be extremely energetic, humane, and considerate, yet he also suffered from depression.[17] Clearly, this greatest ruler of the Mughal Empire was a complex man.

But Akbar was no more complex than the situation he inherited. Ethnically, the territory of the Mughal Empire contained Turks, Mongols, and Uzbeks (these three known collectively as Turanis), as well as hundreds of independent or semi-independent Hindu rulers (rajas). Some of these were territorial chieftains and others were the heads of large families, or clans. Those noblemen expected virtual independence and were reluctant to take orders from any central authority, while the Turks who had come from Persia, or Iran, were often skilled bureaucrats used to working in a strongly centralized administration. Both of these groups were composed of Muslims who viewed Hindus as polytheistic "idolaters."[18] When Akbar came to the throne, his territory was quite small; it consisted of a small crescent of land extending from central Afghanistan through the heart of modern Pakistan down to the north central Indian cities of Panipat and Delhi. By the end of his reign, Akbar's empire contained all of north and central India, including the Indus and Ganges river valleys.

Creating and maintaining a large empire inhabited by such varied ethnic groups required a variety of skills. Akbar needed large armies composed of infantry with firearms, artillery, mounted archers, and elephants. The young ruler spent most of the 1560s and 1570s subduing the Hindu (Rajput) kingdoms in central India from coast to coast. In 1580 and 1581, he put down revolts by family members seeking his throne and others in Kabul and elsewhere in the north taking advantage of Sunni Muslim discontent with his religious and administrative policies. Akbar was unable to finish his military consolidation of the empire until 1601, four years before his death.[19]

In the beginning of his career, Akbar was a skilled military leader intent on increasing his power by enlarging his empire. Until the mid-1570s, he was also a traditional Muslim ruler, subduing the armies of Hindu Rajputs in the name of Allah. But, even in his twenties he began to see both personal and political reasons for some changes in social and religious policy. In 1562, he married the daughter of the Rajput ruler of Jaipur after that kingdom submitted to Mughal overlordship. He was the first Mughal ruler to add Hindu princesses (he later married three more) to his harem and to allow them to maintain their religion. The following year, he dropped the Mughal practice of enslaving the families of defeated enemies, and in 1563 he stopped taxing Hindu pilgrimages. Akbar also ended the traditional tax levied on non-Muslims in 1564, a more radical step, since this tax was levied in all Islamic countries.

Since Akbar remained a devout Muslim during these early years, these policy changes were made largely for political reasons, to win the support of the Rajput rulers. However, Akbar's own religious views and practices were beginning to change. In 1562, he became so impressed by the simple life and wisdom of Muslim mystic Shaikh Salim Chishti that he made a pilgrimage to his shrine each year for seventeen years and even built a new capital, Fatehpur-Sikri, near this site. Shaikh Salim correctly predicted that the emperor, who had difficulty having sons, would have three sons; when the first was born, Akbar named him Salim in honor of the Shaikh. In 1575, the emperor constructed a special building, the Ibadat Khana, in which he brought together thinkers from various religions to discuss the beliefs and practices of each. A Portuguese Jesuit priest, arriving at the court in 1580, recorded this speech by Akbar:

> I perceive that there are varying customs and beliefs of varying religious paths. . . . But the followers of each religion regard the institution of their own religion as better than those of any other. Not only so, but they strive to convert the rest to their own way of belief. If these refuse to be converted, they not only despise them, but also regard them as . . . enemies. And this caused me to feel many serious doubts and scruples. Wherefore I desire that on appointed days the books of all the religious laws be brought forward, and the doctors meet and hold discussions, so that I may hear them, and that each one may determine which is the truest and mightiest religion.[20]

Muslim historians were critical of Akbar's religious policy, which had moved him away from traditional practices by the 1580s, but they admit that he was "deeply religious by nature" and had a soul which "longed for direct spiritual experience." In 1578, Akbar had what has been described as a mystical experience, or "ecstasy," during a royal hunt. He freed all the animals that had been rounded up for him to kill, distributed a large sum of gold to the poor, and cut off his long hair.[21] By 1579, discouraged by Muslim clerical intolerance, he issued a decree that gave him the authority to resolve religious disputes; his decisions would be "binding upon all the people, provided always that such an order is not opposed to the . . . explicit injunction of the Qur'an."[22]

Akbar's beliefs matured quickly. In 1582 he established the *Din-i-Ilahi,* usually translated as "Divine Faith." Its members vowed to dedicate their property, life, and honor to Akbar, espoused a simple monotheism, and renounced "traditional and imitative" Islam. Akbar borrowed rituals from those of the Parsees, Christians, and Hindus. There were initiation ceremonies, feasts on members' birthdays, and a form of bowing to the emperor previously reserved for prayer in the mosque.[23]

Historians disagree on whether or not *Din-i-Ilahi* was a "new" religion (something assumed by many history textbooks) or a way to appeal to non-Muslims and to focus loyalty on the emperor. Many traditional Muslims, led by court scholar Abdul Qadir Badauni, were bitterly critical of the "Divine Faith," which was supported and directed by Abul Fazl, Akbar's chief counselor, famous flatterer, and court historian. Some Muslim historians today see *Din-i-Ilahi* as a superficial form of emperor worship, forbidden by the Qur'an, which undermined the Muslim character of Akbar's state. More "secular" historians praise the emperor for a religious and social policy which, because it was accepting of many traditions, was far ahead of its time. It did not make loyalty to the state dependent on being a member of any official state religion, including Islam; membership in *Din-i-Ilahi* itself was voluntary and somewhere between two dozen and two thousand (sources vary significantly) noblemen joined.[24]

To better evaluate Akbar's religious policy, we need to understand that his administrative system combined features of the personal relations between rulers and their chief nobles found in early feudalism with the practices of a modern government which employs paid officials who feel more of an obligation to the institutions of government than they do to the ruler. Akbar chose his leading civil and military appointees, known as *mansabdars* [Persian for "office-holder"; *mansab* is an "office"], on the basis of their loyalty to him. They were organized into grades, based on how many troops and horses they were expected to supply to Akbar in time of war. To provide the *mansabdars* with money to help them meet this demand, they were assigned revenue from land (*jagirs*). The emperor retained control of all land and could "fire" *mansabdars* and promote or demote them to higher or lower ranks. Akbar divided his empire into twelve large provinces, each led by a governor, who, aided by other officials, administered justice, collected revenue, recruited troops, and kept order. The whole system was reinforced by spies who reported to the court.[25] In 1572–1573 Akbar introduced "branding regulations" (*dagh*) requiring *mansabdars* to present their troops and horses for muster (only the horses were branded) to prove that they were using their money to actually pay troops and not for other, non-military, purposes. By the end of the decade, strict implementation of the *dagh*—along with Akbar's *mahzar* and other religious changes—led some of the Turani *mansabdars* to revolt. After that, he eased the enforcement of the branding regulation.[26]

Some scholars see no connection between Akbar's religious policies (his ending of religious taxes and promoting of "universal peace" and the "Divine Faith") and the loyalty of his military and civilian officials. Others disagree and say that the emperor's "liberal religious ideas" were linked to his imperial system of administration. Akbar changed an empire that had been previously ruled by and for Muslims into one in which Hindu Rajputs could and did play a major role. He favored Hindus as much as he could because he could not always depend upon the loyalty of the Turkish and Mongol nobility. Also, by respecting non-Muslim religions, praising the ideal of "universal peace," and marrying Hindu princesses, Akbar, some say, "transformed" the nobility "into a constructive force" and helped erase the "foreign character of the Mughal Empire." From Akbar's time, the Mughal ruling class no longer saw theirs as *only* a Muslim Empire. Muslims continued to hold the majority of the *mansabs,* but the holders of power in the provinces defined themselves as Mughal *mansabdars,* not as mere servants of a Muslim ruling class. Akbar's court rituals, his use of Hindu *mansabdars,* and the *Din-i-Ilahi* created the impression "not [of] Muslims ruling over Hindus but [of] Muslims and Hindus together, serving a ruler who, whatever his personal beliefs, was not merely a Muslim or Hindu." The empire lasted as long as this practice.[27]

Both Elizabeth I of England and Akbar, the "greatest" Mughal, used a hybrid, or "mixed," religion to try to unify their divided states and promote loyalty to the ruler, and each had personal as well as political motives. Elizabeth's personal religious views, considered "heretical" by Catholics and too "Papist" by the Puritans, were nevertheless those of a sincere Protestant Christian; Akbar's personal views, to the extent that we can determine, given the controversy that surrounds them, were those of a sincere seeker after religious truth who clearly disliked the claims to exclusive truth advanced by Muslim theologians.

In both sixteenth-century England and India, the religion of the ruler did matter. Elizabeth's attempt to create a distinctive "Church of England" that was neither Catholic nor Calvinist suffered a severe setback forty-six years after her death, when the English beheaded Charles I in 1649 and established a Puritan commonwealth under Oliver Cromwell. Akbar's *Din-i-Ilahi* disappeared soon after his death, but his mixed Muslim and Hindu Mughal Empire survived much longer. Religion could be a unifying as well as a divisive force in this period. Perhaps "the religion of the ruler" can only truly become "the religion of the people" in situations in which the ruler's beliefs are only slightly out of step with the beliefs of the majority of his or her subjects. The "Church of England" still exists because Elizabeth did not overreach herself; she was in touch with the sentiment of her people, who would tolerate only a limited amount of religious regulation. The Puritans offered more of this than the English, in the final analysis, would tolerate. Akbar's *Din-i-Ilahi* evaporated after his death because an attempt to join an "inclusive" faith such as Hinduism with an "exclusive" one such as Islam has never succeeded, at least not for long. Akbar's failure perhaps foreshadows that of twentieth-century Indian leader, Mohandas Gandhi, who wished for Hindus and Muslims to live in peace after gaining independence from the British. Gandhi was assassinated in 1947 by a Hindu fanatic. Akbar was spared this fate; only his bones were dug up and burned by an angry mob some fifty years after his death.

Notes

1. Percival Spear, *India: A Modern History*, New Edition, revised and enlarged (Ann Arbor: University of Michigan Press, 1972), 128. Though included in a chapter on Akbar, Spear's statement also specifically refers to Elizabeth as having this quality.
2. Wallace MacCaffrey, *Elizabeth I* (London: Edward Arnold, 1993), 9–10.
3. Jasper Ridley, *Elizabeth I: The Shrewdness of Virtue* (New York: Viking Penguin, 1988), 41, 47–59, 66–67.
4. MaCaffrey, *Elizabeth I*, 48–51; see also Ridley, *Elizabeth*, 33, on her "sincere devotion to the Protestant religion."
5. Carole Levin, *The Heart and Stomach of a King: Elizabeth I and the Politics of Sex and Power* (Philadelphia: University of Pennsylvania Press, 1994), 14.
6. Carl S. Meyer, *Elizabeth I and the Religious Settlement of 1559* (St. Louis: Concordia, 1960), 39, 45–48.
7. See William Haller, *Elizabeth I and the Puritans* (Ithaca, NY: Cornell University Press, 1964), 1–2, 9–10, 21.

8. William P. Haugaard, *Elizabeth and the English Reformation: The Struggle for a Stable Settlement of Religion* (Cambridge: Cambridge University Press, 1968), 78, 248–252; Susan Doran, *Elizabeth I and Religion* (London: Routledge, 1994), 18–19; Meyer, *Religious Settlement*, 149–167.

9. Haugaard, *Elizabeth and the English Reformation*, 25.

10. MacCaffrey, *Elizabeth I*, 300.

11. Joel Hurtsfield, *Elizabeth I and the Unity of England* (London: English Universities Press, 1960), 57.

12. Ridley, *Elizabeth I: Shrewdness of Virtue*, 119–123, 206–214; MacCaffrey, *Elizabeth I*, 202–205; Hurtsfield, *Elizabeth I and Unity of England*, 103.

13. MacCaffrey, *Elizabeth I*, 360–362; Carolly Erickson, *The First Elizabeth* (New York: Summit Books, 1983), 172–173, 313–314.

14. MacCaffrey, *Elizabeth I*, 376–377; Hurstfield, *Elizabeth and Unity of England*, 157. On the reasons Elizabeth may not have married, see Susan Bassnett, *Elizabeth I: A Feminist Perspective* (New York: Berg, 1988), 2–11, which contains a good summary of the speculation and theories of various historians.

15. S. M. Burke, *Akbar. The Greatest Mogul* (New Delhi: Munshiram Monoharlal Publishers, 1989), 17–25, 39–42, contains a clear account of Akbar's youth and the period of Bairam Khan's regency. See also Ashirbadilal Srivastava, *The History of India (1000 AD–1707 AD)* (Agra: Shiva Lal Agarwala, 1964), 469.

16. Burke, *Akbar*, 32; Khaliq Ahmed Nizami, *Akbar and Religion* (Delhi: Idarah-i-Adabiyat, 1989), 1.

17. Burke, *Akbar*, 58, 104–105; Srivastava, *History of India*, 447; Athar Abbas Rizvi, *Religious and Intellectual History of the Muslims in Akbar's Reign* (New Delhi: Munshiram Manoharlal Publishers, 1975), 110; Nizami, *Akbar and Religion*, 2, 165; Muni Lal, *Akbar* (New Delhi: Vikas, 1980), 64, 94, 128, 144–145.

18. Ahsan Raza Khan, *Chieftains in the Mughal Empire* (Simla; Indian Institute Of Advanced Study, 1977), 1–5; Douglas E. Streusand, *The Formation of the Mughal Empire* (Delhi: Oxford University Press, 1989), 23, 26–32.

19. The most convenient summary of Akbar's conquests is in Srivastava, *History of India*, 447–464.

20. Rizvi, *Religious and Intellectual History*, 126–131; Burke, *Akbar*, 102–103. The Ibadat Khana was misnamed the "House of Worship" by earlier historians. It was not a place of worship but a debating hall. For the attitude of the Jesuit missionaries toward Akbar, and their expectations that he would become a Christian, see the fascinating *Letters from the Mughal Court: The First Jesuit Mission to Akbar (1580–83)*, ed. John Corveia-Afonso (St. Louis: Institute of Jesuit Sources, 1981).

21. Nizami, *Akbar and Religion*, is the modern historian most critical of Akbar's religious experiments, believing they constituted an unnecessary departure from traditional Islam that separated him from the "Muslim masses"; see pp. 2, 159–160, 232, 245–246. See also the similar views of Ishtiaq H. Qureshi, in *Akbar: Architect of the Mughal Empire* (Karachi: Ma'aref Ltd., 1978), 165–166. See Burke, *Akbar*, 104, on Akbar's "ecstasy."

22. Rizvi, *Religious and Intellectual History*, 147.

23. Spear, *India: A Modern History*, 135; Burke, *Akbar*, 122–125.

24. Srivastava, *Akbar the Great*, vol. II (Agra: Shiva Lal Agarwala Publishers, 1967), 313–315, sees *Din-i-Ilahi* as "not a religion" but "a common religious bond for at least the elite of the various sections of India's population"; it was designed to promote imperial unity. See also his *History of India*, 474–475, 526–529; Burke, *Akbar*, 122–129, agrees with Srivastava that "Divine Faith" was not a religion but a Sufi brotherhood; it had no scripture, places of worship, or organization of clergy and was not promulgated among the population at large. Nizami, *Akbar and Religion*, 133, 191–193, 215–216, 243–245, 339–340, sees *Din-i-Ilahi* as a new religion, if a weak one, based on a "haphazard agglomeration of certain rituals, whimsically visualized and pompously demonstrated," and designed to improperly make Akbar a "prophet-king." Qureshi, *Akbar: Architect*, 166, agrees with Nizami that *Din-i-Ilahi* was an ill-conceived attempt to promote loyalty to the ruler; it only alienated the "natural [Muslim] supporters of the Empire." Badauni's attack on Akbar, written in 1595–1596, just before his death, is entitled *Muntakhab-ut-Tawarikh* ("History with a Vengeance"); see Harbans Mukhia, *Historians and Historiography During the Reign of Akbar* (New Delhi: Vikas, 1976) for a thorough analysis of Badauni.

25. See Stephen P. Blake, "The Patrimonial-Bureaucratic Empire of the Mughals," in *The State in India*, ed. Hermann Kulke (Delhi: Oxford University Press, 1995), 278–303; for a description of Akbar's military and the *mansabdari* system, see Srivastava, *Akbar the Great*, II, 217–247; Streusand, *Formation of the Mughal Empire*, 139–148.

26. See Streusand, *Formation of the Mughal Empire*, 154–172, on Akbar's "crisis and compromise."

27. Among those who see little connection between Akbar's religious policy and his success as an imperial ruler is Khan, *Chieftains in the Mughal Empire*, 222–23, who says that Akbar's military "striking capacity" and ability to punish rebels, and not his "liberal religious ideas," kept people loyal; see also Iqtidar Alam Khan, "The Nobility Under Akbar and the Development of His Religious Policy, 1560–80" *Journal of the Royal Asiatic Society of Great Britain and Ireland* (1968; parts

I & II): 29–36, who believes that Akbar's religious concessions to non-Muslims were tactical devices in response to the hostility of the conservative Muslims, and not part of a broader vision of a multi-religious Mughal Empire. The more common view, that his religious policy did matter, is expressed by P. S. Bedi, *The Mughal Nobility Under Akbar* (Jalandhar: ABS Publications, 1985), vii, 22, and in Streusand, *Formation of the Mughal Empire,* 123–153.

Further Reading

BURKE, S. M. *Akbar, the Greatest Mogul.* New Delhi: Munshiram Monoharlal Publishers, 1989. This brief biography of the ruler tries to strike a balance between Hindu and Muslim historians and is written from a modern Western perspective.

DORAN, SUSAN. *Elizabeth I and Religion.* London: Routledge, 1994. A clear, brief account which summarizes much of the research of the past thirty years.

MACCAFFREY, WALLACE. *Elizabeth I.* London: Edward Arnold, 1993. Thoughtful, readable biography.

NIZAMI, KHALIQ AHMED. *Akbar and Religion.* Delhi: Idarah-i-Adabiyat-i-Delhi, 1989. Written by a Muslim scholar hostile to the *Din-i-Ilahi* who offers some good reasons this faith did not last.

CHAPTER 15

Kangxi and Louis XIV: Dynastic Rulers, East and West

To what extent can dynastic rulers control their own fate? What is the key to successful "absolutism"?

In the world of the late seventeenth century, a comparison between Kangxi and Louis XIV is an obvious one. At opposite ends of the Eurasian land mass, these two rulers clearly stand out. In western Europe, Louis XIV (1638–1715), a member of France's Bourbon dynasty, ruled that continent's most powerful nation. In the Far East, Kangxi (1654–1722), a member of the Qing [pronounced "ching"] dynasty, was emperor of China.[1] Both rulers had equally long reigns. Kangxi's years of personal rule lasted from 1669 to 1722 (fifty-three years and four major wars), while those of Louis XIV extended from 1661 to 1715 (fifty-four years and the same number of wars).

Given their longevity, it is not surprising that each man experienced personal tragedies. Son and grandsons preceded Louis XIV in death, so that a five-year-old great-grandson, Louis XV, was left as successor in 1715. Kangxi's oldest son and "heir apparent," Yinreng, was infamous for his acts of sexual depravity, sadism, and irresponsibility. After years of fatherly patience, sorrow, and cover-ups, Kangxi declared him mad and then deposed and arrested him in 1712.[2] These family problems were also political ones, for the success of dynastic government depends upon the quality of the ruler. In the Chinese case, Kangxi's fourth son, Yinzhen, proved to be a far more capable ruler than the original heir apparent would have been. The French were less fortunate; Louis XV proved to be a lazy and mistress-ridden monarch. The Qing dynasty lasted until

1911; the Bourbon dynasty collapsed in the storm of the French Revolution (1789–1799).

The great energy and determination that both Kangxi and Louis XIV displayed clearly distinguish them from their successors. Kangxi's writings frequently note the importance of hard work and attention to detail. "This is what we have to do," he wrote, "apply ourselves to human affairs to the utmost, while remaining responsive to the dictates of Heaven. In agriculture, one must work hard in the fields *and* hope for fair weather." Louis also relished the hard work necessary to run a large state. In notes he wrote for his successor, he warned against "prolonged idleness" and advised that a regular work schedule was good for the spirit: "No satisfaction can equal that of following each day the progress of glorious and lofty undertakings and of the happiness of the people, when one has planned it all himself."[3] Both rulers felt personally responsible for the welfare of their subjects, yet both fought major wars to extend their lands and their power. Since warfare was expensive in money and lives, it was not always easy for these men to balance their desire for power with their desire to improve the lives of their subjects.

This very tension between war and peace helps illuminate some of the problems facing even a conscientious autocratic, or "absolute," ruler during these last few centuries before the world was transformed forever by the Industrial Revolution. Neither Louis XIV nor Kangxi had to please voters or make decisions about social and economic programs, with one ear cocked to a national stock market or an international monetary system. Their job was simpler—in theory, anyway. It was to strengthen the power of their dynasty by maintaining the military and economic strength of their country. The precise way in which each ruler pursued this goal tells us something about China and western Europe and something of the pitfalls facing an "absolute" ruler in the days before telephones, fax machines and computers.

Kangxi was a Manchu. That fact defined his political task. The warlike Manchu nomads, who lived northeast of China, had gradually increased their territory and power at the expense of the Ming dynasty, which ruled China from 1368 to 1644. In the early seventeenth century, Manchu leader Nurhaci (1559–1626) began to transform the Manchu tribes into a modern state by curbing the power of local chiefs and by centralizing the government. His sons continued this process of consolidation, and the Manchus thus were able to conquer Beijing easily in 1644, once the last Ming emperor was defeated and committed suicide. Kangxi's father, the first Qing emperor, needed to win support from native Chinese leaders, especially the Confucian scholars. To accomplish this, he appointed two men to all top-level government positions, one a Manchu and the other a native [or Han] Chinese. Throughout his long reign, Kangxi continued his father's balance in making all major appointments so that native Chinese would not unduly resent their foreign leaders. This proved wise, since the Manchus, while militarily superior to the Chinese in the beginning of the reign, were vastly outnumbered. To govern China successfully, a foreign dynasty had to have so much native help in ruling that it became virtually Chinese.[4]

Kangxi was only seven years old in 1661 when his father died, leaving the government to four noblemen assigned to govern on his behalf. Although Kangxi ended this regency in 1667, it was two years later before he was able to break the power of one particularly powerful regent. When the fifteen-year-old ruler acted, he did so decisively, throwing the offending overmighty subject, Oboi, into prison, where he died five years later.[5]

By acting decisively and wisely and appearing strong, Kangxi strengthened his own personal power and that of his empire. He increased the army's size from one hundred eighty-five thousand men in 1661 to three hundred fifteen thousand in 1684. He took up to seventy thousand of them north of the Great Wall two or three times a year on hunting trips (really military maneuvers), so that they might keep their archery and riding sharp. He appointed former Manchu army leaders as provincial governors. In 1667, such appointees governed twenty-eight of the twenty-nine provinces. Kangxi also shrewdly conducted frequent audiences with military leaders; he believed that a general who occasionally bowed to the emperor remained humble and "properly fearful."[6]

By the middle of his reign, Kangxi's wise choice of subordinates, realistic understanding of people, and close attention to detail reduced the danger of rebellion by unhappy Chinese subjects or discontented Manchu clan leaders. Before this happened, however, the emperor had to fight a bloody and prolonged war against three rebel leaders in the south. This war began in 1673 and lasted until 1682, in part because the emperor had trouble finding good generals. After defeating the three rebel states, Kangxi was able to add the island of Taiwan to his empire in 1684. It was more difficult to establish Chinese power firmly in the north. This took major campaigns against the Russians and against the Mongol chieftain, Galdan.

Before moving to dislodge the Russians from Chinese territory along the Amur River, where they had been settling since the 1650s, Kangxi made his usual careful preparations. He collected enough military supplies for a three-year war and moved Dutch-designed cannons and men trained to use them to the front. In 1685, he captured the Russian fortress at Albazin, and in 1689 the Treaty of Nerchinsk restored Chinese control in the area.[7] It took eight more years for Kangxi to defeat the western Mongol tribes led by Galdan. "Now my purpose is accomplished, my wishes fulfilled," the elated emperor wrote when a defeated Galdan committed suicide in 1697. "Isn't this the will of Heaven? I am so extremely happy!" These western victories set the stage for Chinese domination of Tibet, which began in the final years of Kangxi's reign and has lasted intermittently to our own day.[8]

Of course, external security was not enough. Dynastic rulers were obliged to keep constant and careful watch over subjects and subordinates. Kangxi did this by devising a system of palace memorials. These secret reports from agents of unquestioned loyalty to the ruler and the dynasty contained detailed information and comments, sent directly to the emperor and viewed by him alone. Their use allowed him to bypass official channels, to learn of official incompetence and would-be plots, and to quickly acquire more accurate information than that provided by the Grand Secretariat.

One of the emperor's most trusted agents was a Manchu bondservant named Cao Yin (1658–1712). This competent administrator had a classical Confucian education and wrote poetry with his Chinese friends in his spare time; he was an ideal informant for Kangxi, who sent him to the city of Nanjing as textile commissioner in 1692. In his role as manager of imperial textile factories, Cao Yin supervised twenty-five hundred artisans and 664 looms, and he shipped quotas of silk to Beijing. In secret palace memorials written between 1697 and his death, he gave the emperor detailed information on the local harvest, problems faced by the local governor, and the "condition of the common people." Another secret memorialist sent reports to the emperor on the movements of 5,923 grain boats that left Yangzhou for Beijing each year. Such information helped the emperor keep his officials honest and stop trouble before it started.[9]

Such close supervision of foodstuffs and silk production was important to a ruler who relied on a closely regulated economy. The textile factories at Nanjing, Hangzhou, and Suzhou were monopolies run by the government, which provided funds and established production quotas. During his reign, Kangxi tried to strengthen these government controls over trade. In 1699, for example, a statute ended private rights to purchase copper and gave the copper monopoly to merchants from the imperial household in Peking.[10] Neither Kangxi nor his French counterpart favored "free enterprise," which they considered inefficient and foolish. In their opinion, the state alone had sufficient wealth to underwrite large commercial projects. These mercantilist rulers also asked why private citizens should enrich themselves with money that could be going to the state and ruler. They also worried that overly rich subjects might be more likely to rebel against their rule.

One of the central features of absolutist government was the clear tendency to link the welfare of a country with the power of its ruler. If this was the case in China, which enjoyed two thousand years of unified government, it was even more true in France. There, in the absence of a long tradition of dynastic government, it was often only the strength of the ruler that prevented the kingdom from breaking into the separate provinces from which it had been created. Louis XIV early learned the need for a strong monarchy; his lesson was as important in shaping French absolutism as was Kangxi's Manchu heritage in shaping Chinese government policies.

In 1648, when Louis was ten, an uprising known as the Fronde forced his mother and her chief minister, Cardinal Mazarin, to flee Paris to avoid capture by hostile armies. Although this uprising was poorly organized and sputtered within a few years, the revolt impressed the young monarch (as did Kangxi's battle with the too powerful regent Oboi) with the need to create both the image and the reality of a strong monarchy. When Louis assumed personal rule in 1661 after the death of Mazarin, he quickly established his authority by refusing to appoint a new chief minister and by arresting Nicholas Fouquet, his extremely wealthy and corrupt finance minister. By hard work, Louis soon convinced others he was the "Sun King"; his palace at Versailles was soon the envy of other European monarchs.

The challenge Louis faced was greater than that which confronted Kangxi, since the former had to create a new tradition; the

Manchu ruler, on the other hand, had only to prove that his new dynasty fit into existing Chinese traditions. For centuries the French nobility had seen the king as only "first among equals." Louis had to change all that, and he did, using some of the same methods as his Chinese contemporary, as well as some unique ones.

Like Kangxi, Louis employed officials loyal to him alone. But these differed from those in China, who were members of an ancient bureaucracy. Since France lacked a traditional bureaucracy, Louis had to build a new bureaucracy on the foundation laid by his father. His objective was to create an administration that allowed him to undercut the power of the old nobility while he strengthened his power at home and abroad. In selecting officials, the young king chose people from France's middle-class—men of dedication and ability, such as Michel Le Tellier as secretary of state for war and Jean-Baptiste Colbert as controller-general of finance. These commoners, like the Manchu bondservants used by Kangxi, had no social or political status other than that conferred on them by their employer; they were loyal servants because they owed everything to the king.

By employing them, the king was able to create a civil and military organization that freed his dynasty from dependence on the old noble families of the realm. Louis's appointment of Colbert, in particular, proved judicious and shows some of the similarities between economic development in Europe and in China. As chief financial official, Colbert attempted to create a strong, state-directed economy designed to make the king strong in France and France strong in Europe. His international goal was a favorable balance of trade. So, while the Chinese were using state factories in Nanjing to produce silk for export to Europe via the Philippine Islands, Colbert was making France as self-sufficient as possible and generating income for the king by exports abroad from government-subsidized silk works at Lyons, linen factories at Arras, and pottery works at Nevers. To curb the import of foreign products into France, Colbert convinced the king to raise tariffs [taxes on foreign goods] in 1664 and 1667.[11] France's adoption of this mercantilist economic system was based on the belief that there was only a limited amount of wealth in the world, and the country that got to it first would prosper the most. Naturally, Colbert encouraged Frenchmen to establish trading colonies overseas, and he strengthened the royal navy and merchant marine in order to make this sort of expansion more attractive. The limited success of Colbert's policies was due to their expense. The tax structure and its collection system could not generate enough revenue to meet military and civilian needs. The French farmed out tax collection to private citizens, or tax farmers, who had to turn in a fixed amount of money to the king but could keep for themselves anything collected beyond that amount. Such a system encouraged graft and placed a great burden on the poor. The fact that Louis was unable to scrap this system in favor of one able to produce more revenue and greater fairness, and the fact that the nobility remained exempt from taxation, show some of the limitations on absolute monarchs in the seventeenth century.

That Louis used Le Tellier's professional army to engage in dynastic wars rather than using his limited funds to promote greater domestic prosperity shows another flaw in the system of absolutism. Dynastic wars reflected the will of a single person, and they served as the quickest path to necessary short-term prestige. Louis chose war, at first to secure glory and territory, and finally in self-defense. The War of Devolution, 1667–1668, was fought to get territory in the Spanish Netherlands [modern Belgium]. It was a limited success but led to the less successful Dutch War of 1672–1678; the Dutch prevented a decisive French victory when they opened the dikes and flooded the territory around Amsterdam. The French did expand their frontiers in both wars, and they used dubious legal claims after 1678 to continue annexations along their eastern border, taking the important fortress city of Strasbourg (then in the Holy Roman Empire) in 1681.

All this, especially when combined with Louis' insufferable vanity (he offered to settle with the Dutch in 1672 if they would strike a gold medal in his honor, thanking him for giving them peace),[12] naturally alarmed Louis' neighbors. When the king moved troops into Germany in 1688, he soon found himself facing a coalition of Germans, Dutch, and English. The War of the League of Augsburg lasted until 1697 and ended in a stalemate. Louis' last war, also fought against many enemies, was the War of the Spanish Succession, 1701–1713. The decision of the French king to place his grandson on the vacant Spanish throne threatened the "balance of power" in Europe by giving the Bourbon dynasty control of two major states. Louis made matters worse by refusing to promise that the two thrones would never be united. The "Sun King" was partly defeated this time. Like the earlier contests, this was a battle for overseas markets as well as political power, with the English fighting to capture French territories across the Atlantic as well as in Europe. The French lost Nova Scotia and Newfoundland to the British in 1713 at the Peace of Utrecht. It was the prelude to further French defeats in the Americas later in that century.

In the final analysis, the wars of Louis XIV damaged his country and his dynasty as much as the wars of Kangxi had strengthened his. In Louis' defense, we should note that neither his armies nor his territorial gains were any greater than those of the Chinese emperor. His pursuit of glory and prestige was probably not as determined as that of Kangxi. The reasons Louis's absolutism was less successful than that of Kangxi are twofold: the Chinese absolutist system was much older and more firmly established than that of France; second, in the absence of strong neighbors, the Chinese did not have to conduct foreign policy (the very term would have seemed strange to Kangxi) in the midst of a system of rival states, each one concerned that none of the others becomes too strong. Kangxi did not have to establish a tradition of strong central government in the face of a hostile aristocracy. He had only to show that he, a Manchu, was fit to sit on the throne of the "Son of Heaven." In addition, Kangxi's foreign enemies were all inferior to him in strength. Finally, there was no "balance of power" in east Asia that the Chinese emperor was expected to maintain; China was the "central country" in east Asia in fact as well as in name.

All this is not to excuse Louis XIV's arrogance or errors of judgment. It was not a good idea, either politically or economically, for Louis to achieve religious unity by allowing his officials to persecute Huguenots [French Protestants] and in 1685 to revoke the Edict of Nantes, which had given them limited religious freedom. As a consequence, a significant number of Louis' most productive subjects fled to other countries, giving the king a bad image. Louis' splendid palace at Versailles did help him control the nobility by skillfully keeping them there in attendance on him. It also awed foreign monarchs and visitors. However, the "splendid isolation" of the dynasty outside of Paris alienated later Bourbon monarchs from their subjects and contributed to the collapse of the monarchy during the French Revolution. While the Chinese emperors might also be accused of "arrogance" by a Westerner (their court ceremonial, for example, was much more elaborate than that of Louis), their "arrogance" was sanctioned by centuries-long traditions. It was, we might say, an institutional rather than a personal arrogance.

It is impossible, then, to evaluate the success or failure of either of these dynasts without taking into account their cultural and historical setting. For the Chinese, Kangxi proved a blessing. After fifty years of turmoil and inefficiency, he brought his subjects a long period of decisive, sensible, efficient rule. In short, he proved himself a conservative restorer of the old.[13] Louis, on the other hand, while considered a conservative by modern standards (how else could a modern student of government view an advocate of one-man rule, sanctioned by God?), was revolutionary in the context of seventeenth-century French and European history. By identifying himself with the state, he helped to shift people's attention to the state as a focus for their primary loyalty.[14] His bureaucratic innovations, and even his wars, helped the French to see their country as more than a collection of provinces. Louis may not get the credit for this, but he did help pave the way for the day when the French would die for "la patrie," the "fatherland." It is one of the ironies of French history that a chief victim of that new spirit of national unity Louis helped create was the Bourbon dynasty that he had worked so hard to strengthen.

Notes

1. Kangxi (spelled K'ang-hsi in older works) was his title, not his personal name. Chinese rulers, much like Roman Catholic popes, took a new name when they began their rule, and so Xuan Ye (this ruler's personal name) became *the* Kangxi emperor. Many historians simplify matters and avoid confusion by using the reign title or name as if it were a personal one. We do the same in this chapter.
2. Silas H. L. Wu, *Passage to Power: K'ang-hsi and His Heir Apparent, 1661–1722* (Cambridge, MA: Harvard University Press, 1979) is an excellent study of the "murderous power struggle" between K'ang-hsi and his son; see a good short summary in Jonathan D. Spence, *The Search for Modern China* (New York: Norton, 1990), 69–71.
3. Jonathan D. Spence, *Emperor of China: Self-Portrait of K'ang-hsi* (New York: Random House 1974), 57; see also 11, 12–13, 47, 58–59, 147; Louis XIV, King of France, *Memoires for the Instruction of the Dauphin,*

translated with an introduction by Paul Sonnino (New York: Free Press, 1970), 29–30.

4. This process by which the Manchu dynasty became both powerful and Chinese is discussed in the first fifty pages of Lawrence D. Kessler, *K'ang-hsi and the Consolidation of Ch'ing Rule, 1661–1684* (Chicago: University of Chicago Press, 1976).

5. Ibid., 65–73.

6. Ibid., 105, 116–118; Spence, *Emperor of China*, 42–43. Governor-generals were military leaders who controlled more than one province.

7. Kessler, *K'ang-hsi*, 100–101.

8. Wu, *Passage to Power*, 65; Spence, *Search for Modern China*, 68.

9. Jonathan D. Spence, *Ts'ao Yin and the K'ang-hsi Emperor, Bondservant and Master* (New Haven: Yale University Press, 1966), 213–254.

10. Ibid., 109–110.

11. Vincent Buranelli, *Louis XIV* (New York: Twayne Publishers, 1966), 72–78.

12. John B. Wolf, *Louis XIV* (New York: Norton, 1968), 224.

13. See Jonathan D. Spence, "The Seven Ages of K'ang-hsi (1654–1722)" *Journal of Asian Studies*, XXVI (February 1967): 205–211.

14. See Roland Mousnier, *Louis XIV*, trans. J. W. Hunt (London: The Historical Association, 1973), 18–25.

Further Reading

LOUIS XIV, KING OF FRANCE, *Memoires for the Instruction of the Dauphin*. Trans. PAUL SONNINO. New York: Free Press, 1970. Louis speaks for himself. Read with care.

SPENCE, JONATHAN D. *Emperor of China: Self-Portrait of K'ang-hsi*. New York: Alfred A. Knopf, 1974. Excellent. Brings this ruler to life.

WOLF, JOHN B. *Louis XIV*. New York: Norton, 1968. Long but readable.